Take the first step in faith.
You don't have to see the whole staircase,
just take the first step.

—Dr. Martin Luther King Jr.

Your present plans are going to succeed.

—Message found inside a fortune cookie
served at a Chinese restaurant
in Morris, Minnesota, in 1999

A Job Search Manual for Counselors and Counselor Educators

How to Navigate and Promote Your Counseling Career

Shannon Hodges ■ Amy Reece Connelly

AMERICAN COUNSELING ASSOCIATION
5999 Stevenson Avenue
Alexandria, VA 22304
www.counseling.org

A Job Search Manual
for Counselors and
Counselor Educators
How to Navigate and Promote Your Counseling Career

10   9   8   7   6   5   4   3   2   1

American Counseling Association
5999 Stevenson Avenue
Alexandria, VA 22304

Director of Publications ■ Carolyn C. Baker

Production Manager ■ Bonny E. Gaston

Editorial Assistant ■ Catherine A. Brumley

Copy Editor ■ Kathleen Porta Baker

Cover and text design by Bonny E. Gaston.

Library of Congress Cataloging-in-Publication Data
Hodges, Shannon.
A job search manual for counselors and counselor educators : how to navigate and promote your counseling career/Shannon Hodges, Amy Reece Connelly.
    p. cm.
Includes bibliographical references and index.
ISBN 978-1-55620-297-1 (alk. paper)
    1. Job hunting—Handbooks, manuals, etc. 2. Résumés (Employment)—Handbooks, manuals, etc.   I. Connelly, Amy Reece.   II. Title.
HF5382.7.H63 2010
650.14—dc22   2009028553

Table of Contents

Preface

This book has taken 20 years to move from conception to birth. In the late 1980s, I was working as a vocational–employment counselor in a large human services agency in Oregon. My job was to provide career and employment counseling to unemployed adolescents and adults, and it included vocational and career testing, career counseling, and teaching classes on interviewing skills and writing cover letters and résumés. I frequently made use of iconic texts such as Richard Nelson Bolles's (2004, 2007) *What Color Is Your Parachute?* and Yana Parker's (2002) *The Damn Good Résumé Guide* as instructional aids. During this time, I began to toy with the idea of writing my own career and job search text, based on my education and practical experience in the field. Although I had all the interest to take on such a project, I had none of the experience to see me through such an undertaking. To complicate matters, I was having difficulty choosing a focus for a career text because, after all, there were numerous such books already on the market.

One day during a lunchtime discussion with another agency counselor, it dawned on me that there might be a place for a niche text focusing on job search and career advice for professional counselors. After all, although counselors were supposedly experts on career search, it seemed to me that many counselors had had very little training and mentoring on how to conduct their own job search. I considered that perhaps I would be the person to write such a book. My book idea even went as far as sketching out possible chapters that would make up the text. But, as it so often does, reality interrupted the process—I was busy with my job and doctoral studies and dealing with all the energy and work that goes into earning a doctorate, in addition to the tribulations of my own job search. Still, I continued to give idle thought to my original idea of writing a career text for counselors.

My idea remained just that until the spring of 2008, when a confluence of events brought me back to seriously examining my original concept for a career book for counselors. At the time, I felt my own career had arrived at another crossroads, and I was confused as to which avenue to take. I was ready to write a professional book but unsure what the book would be. I had also been contemplating a move overseas, and I wondered about the counseling job market outside the United States but could find little guidance on the matter.

As I considered various options for the direction of my career, it dawned on me that the time was ripe to write the career text that had dogged my thoughts for two decades. I believed my own experience, though, was incomplete and that I needed a coauthor with strengths to compensate for my areas of weakness. Several years earlier, I had met Amy Reece Connelly when she worked as the manager of career services for the American Counseling Association. I had been impressed with her knowledge, energy, and depth of experience in the career field. I contacted her and inquired whether she would be interested in working with me on this text. She gave me an enthusiastic "Yes!" During the past year, we have worked closely to ensure we have covered the major issues related to both job search and career enhancement for counselors and counselor educators.

Naturally, counseling is not a monolithic career; many different types of counseling, counseling organizations, and professional counseling divisions exist. No career text could possibly cover all issues and contingencies within the broad field of professional counseling. We believe, however, that we have created a comprehensive manual to provide counselors and counselor educators with important job search information that will assist them in their career journey. In this book, we have covered the basics regarding the job market, networking, writing résumés and curricula vitae, assessing the pros and cons of self-employment, and managing job rejection and disappointment. We have also made numerous recommendations on how to improve your chances of landing the job you desire. Of course, we understand readers will agree with many of our suggestions and disagree with others. This is natural and probably a good sign because counselors have learned much valuable information through the crucible of their graduate education, years of experience, and what my former Ozark neighbor, friend, and 40-year teacher Grace Hunt referred to as the "college of hard knocks" (life). We encourage you to use our text to build on your already existing wealth of knowledge and improve your chances as you seek the job and career you desire. Although we believe we have authored a very good book, this text itself is no substitute for career counseling. It can, however, serve as additional, helpful information.

Amy and I also wish you good fortune and fulfillment during your career journey.

—*Shannon Hodges*
Burlington, VT

Acknowledgments

I heard somewhere that writing a book is a lot like childbirth.

Having experienced both processes now, I will affirm that there are many similarities. In the case of *this* book, my friend, colleague, and writing partner Shannon Hodges and I, independently of one another, each had a "pregnant" thought for a job search manual targeted toward those in the counseling profession. When Shannon approached me in the spring of 2008 to partner with him on this project, I welcomed his vast experience as a counselor educator and practicing counselor, which complemented my focus as a career consultant and marketing strategist.

Much like determined parents-to-be, we developed a plan, excited about what each of us would bring to the project. Once "conception" occurred (i.e., the contract was signed), we were committed, and despite some very interesting and unexpected changes in the global economy, and in our own professional lives, there was no turning back.

Within a couple of months, Shannon had produced a first draft, which he entrusted to me to nurture and carry through to completion. He has been a perfect "birth partner," encouraging me in this undertaking that I had always carried in my conscious and subconscious and that simultaneously both thrilled and terrified me, leaving me somewhat guilt-ridden at times.

During the writing process, I had a few thoughts along the lines of "Dear God, what have I gotten myself into?" "I can't believe I agreed to this," and "What if I can't live up to the expectations?" All of these thoughts were accompanied by the nausea, panic, high blood pressure, and heartburn associated with gestation.

As we approached the due date, the desire to deliver grew, and there seemed to be greater anticipation of how our "offspring" would be received. Shannon's concerned prodding and my own drive prompted by fear of failure (I am, after all, an ENTJ) somehow got us through the final weeks, along with heavy doses of encouragement from my real-life partner, husband Kevin, who talked me down from the ledge on more than one occasion, and my daughters, Kristine and Kara, who regularly brought me cookies and milk for midafternoon writing breaks. My sister, Emily, and parents, David and Judi, could also be counted on for editing, reality checks, and occasional (loving) kicks in the pants.

I dedicate this finished product to my two writing grandmothers—Cleota, whose personal poetry and letters from the heart inspired me at an early age and encouraged me through young motherhood, and Sady, whose pioneering advertising and marketing career demonstrated to me, firsthand, that women really can have it all if they prepare carefully and plan appropriately—and to their life partners, my wonderful grandfathers—Charles, whose kind dedication to mission and helping others was deeply instilled in our family, and Bill, whose memorable sense of humor was always accompanied by a good balance of practicality and common sense. I hope I've inherited the best of all of them.

Finally, in the spirit of my own culture, I offer this text for "baptism," pledging it to the service of Our Creator, in the ardent hope that He will use it for the good of His people.

And now, I'm going to celebrate, have some champagne, catch up on some sleep (thankfully, in this process sleep deprivation comes before the birth), schedule a spa day, and lose the "baby weight" I've picked up over the course of this project.

—Amy Reece Connelly

■

For better than a decade I have toyed with the idea of writing a career search text focused solely on the counseling profession. But because good intentions are all too frequently just that, I let the idea percolate until March 2008. Finally, one morning while staring through my Niagara University office window at Canada just across the Niagara River gorge, it dawned on me that it was time to start writing this text. Once I began, it almost seemed that the text wrote itself because my ideas seemed to flow naturally from my mind to the keyboard and onto the screen. I am proud of the work Amy and I have produced because it is the first career search manual to address solely the counseling profession.

Several people were instrumental in encouraging my progress on this project: my spouse Shoshanna, who always encourages me to strive toward my dreams; my grandparents, who instilled in me the value of education; and my colleague Kris Augustyniak, who was there to provide a listening ear (and at times, a metaphorical kick in the pants!).

Finally, my part of this text is dedicated to the memory of the late Reese House. Although a busy, influential Oregon State University professor of counselor education, he somehow found it worthwhile to mentor a seemingly unpromising graduate student from rural Arkansas. Even after I completed my doctorate, Reese continued to encourage and challenge me to become a professor of counselor education. Whenever I needed a referral, a reality check, or just a friendly listening ear, he was there. It is mainly because of his careful cultivation that I have cowritten this text. Reese was an outstanding teacher, a worthy role model, an advocate of social justice, and one of the most compassionate people I have been privileged to meet. *Reese, I hold your memory in the light.*

—*Shannon Hodges*

About the Authors

Shannon Hodges, PhD, LMHC, NCC, is an associate professor of clinical mental health counseling and director of clinical education at Antioch University New England. He has experience as a director of a university counseling center, director of a county mental health clinic, including 16 years experience in community mental health, several years experience in college student services, and more than 20 years experience teaching job search skills, résumé writing, and interviewing in higher education and community agencies. Throughout his professional career, he has had extensive experience serving on job search committees. Shannon also serves as an associate of Shoshanna Cogan, Inc., a private global consulting and training firm providing consulting and training in diversity education, mediation, visioning, and professional coaching to nonprofit agencies and international organizations. He is a longtime member of the American Counseling Association, the American Mental Health Counselors Association, and several American Counseling Association divisional affiliates. Shannon has also authored books, book chapters, journal articles, poetry, and essays.

■

Amy Reece Connelly, MA, is the CEO of Connelly & Associates, Inc., an Indiana-based consulting firm specializing in career development programs for associations and individuals, and global services team leader for Ricklin-Echikson Associates, an international human resources consulting firm. Previously, from 2003 to 2008, she was the manager of career services for the American Counseling Association and wrote *Your Coun-*

seling Career, a monthly column in *Counseling Today*. She has 20 years of experience in front-line career development, having been employed as a career counselor in a university setting, an executive recruiter, and a provider of outplacement services. She is a member of the American Counseling Association, the American Association of Christian Counselors, the National Employment Counseling Association, and the National Career Development Association, where she is designated as a Master Career Development Professional.

Preparing to Enter the Job Search Market

The future belongs to those who believe in the beauty of their dreams.
—Eleanor Roosevelt

Many job seekers believe that a résumé and a navy blue suit are all they need to be successful in the job market. Although a résumé (or in some cases, a curriculum vitae) is, necessarily, a key component of an effective campaign, your interview suit might hang in the closet for a long time if you don't recognize the other crucial elements of a successful job search.

This may be your first time in the job market or your 20th. You may be looking for a survival job, a transition job, or your dream job. Whatever your desired outcome, we encourage you to recognize that every effective job search begins with an analysis of your strengths and marketability.

In this chapter, we discuss the steps necessary to successfully prepare for a job search, including

- finding the types of jobs appropriate for your level of experience;
- using the job search as a means of long-term career planning;
- determining the tools you'll need to conduct a successful job search;
- evaluating your skills to enable you to communicate them to potential employers; and
- identifying and prioritizing what you seek in your work to guide your application process.

Self-Assessment

Most career development professionals encourage candidates in the job market to begin with a good self-assessment, which includes a critical evaluation of their skills, interests, and values. Because you are reading *this* book, we assume that you have the interests and skills necessary to be a good counselor. (Why else would you have spent several years and thousands of dollars preparing for this career field?)

Are Your Skills the Same as Every Other Counselor's Skills?

Consider your cohort for a moment. Are you exactly like every other counselor with whom you attended classes? Of course not. Although you probably share some core interests, skills, and values, you are an individual with interests, skills, and values that set you apart even from those who are in your career field. Those diverse interests and skills will help you to differentiate yourself from every other counselor who will join you in the job market.

Here are some examples:

- Do you speak a second (or third, fourth, or fifth) language? This particular skill may be advantageous for counseling positions in geographic areas in which a concentrated population speaks that language.
- Do you have a background in business? Counselors who can read financial reports and manage budgets are often in demand for management positions.
- Are you an effective speaker? Many nonprofit agencies need people who can do outreach activities to support marketing and development efforts.

What Other Skills Do You Possess That Set You Apart From Others in Your Chosen Profession?

Counseling is not a cookie-cutter career. This profession draws people from all walks of life. We know people who have entered this profession as a second career after having been attorneys, teachers, mechanics, artists, flight attendants, sales representatives, military officers, advertising executives, and physicians, to name just a few of the diverse backgrounds. That makes a lot of sense because effective counseling depends on good communication between the counselor and the client. Diversity in the field ensures that there are counselors who can relate to every population.

Our goal in this book is to help you identify for yourself and communicate to potential employers how you can be an asset to various organizations in which counseling is a key component.

Job Prospects for Counselors

Before proceeding, let's take a look at the employment outlook for the field of counseling and the types of jobs available.

The positive news is that the occupational outlook for most counseling specialty fields is very good and "expected to grow much faster than the average for all occupations through 2016" (U.S. Department of Labor, 2008, p. 209); however, the job market for counselors varies by location and counseling specialty field. Still, job prospects should remain strong as the result of growth and the need to replace counselors leaving the field.

Overall, employment of counselors is expected to grow by 21% between 2006 and 2016 (see Table 1.1), which is much faster than the average for all occupations (U.S. Department of Labor, 2008). Employment of substance abuse counselors is expected to grow by 34%, which makes this the fastest growing of all mental health occupations (U.S. Department of Labor, 2008). Employment of school counselors is expected to grow by about 13%, about the same as for most professional occupations (U.S. Department of Labor, 2008). Job growth may change depending on future changes in governmental funding. Employment of mental health counselors is expected to grow by 30%, much faster than the average for all occupations (U.S. Department of Labor, 2008). Job growth for rehabilitation counselors is projected to grow by 23%, faster than average (U.S. Department of Labor, 2008).

Here are relevant 2006 statistics, as reported by the U.S. Department of Labor (2008) for the employment of counselors:

Educational, vocational, and school counselors	260,000
Rehabilitation counselors	141,000
Mental health counselors	100,000
Substance abuse and behavioral disorder counselors	83,000
Marriage and family counselors–therapists	25,000
Counselors, all others (including creative arts counselors)	27,000
Total number of counselors in all areas of counseling	635,000

Earnings for Counselors

The median salary for counselors varies, depending on the counseling specialty; geographic region; urban, suburban, or rural setting; level of educa-

Table 1.1
Projections for Counselor Occupational Growth, 2006–2016

Occupational Title	2006 Employment	Projected 2016 Employment	Projected Increase	Projected % Increase
Total no. counselors	636,000	771,000	135,000	21
By counseling specialty				
Substance abuse and behavioral disorder	83,000	112,000	29,000	34
Educational, vocational, and school	260,000	292,000	33,000	13
Marriage and family	25,000	32,000	7,400	30
Mental health	100,000	130,000	30,000	30
Rehabilitation	141,000	173,000	32,000	23
All other counselors	27,000	32,000	4,500	17

Note. Statistics for individual specialty and total are reported as they appear in U.S. Department of Labor (2008) and may not sum correctly.

tion; and so forth. The U.S. Department of Labor (2008, p. 210) reported the following statistics regarding counselor salaries:

Elementary and secondary school counselors	$53,750
Colleges, universities, and professional schools	$41,780
Community and junior colleges	$48,240
Social service agencies	$32,370
Vocational rehabilitation services	$31,340
Mental health counselors	$34,380
Rehabilitation counselors	$29,200
Addictions counselors	$34,040
Marriage and family counselors–therapists	$43,210
Counselors, other	Not listed

(U.S. Department of Labor, 2008, p. 210)

The Three Types of Jobs and How to Transition Through Them

People in the job market represent all elements of society, and the types of jobs they seek are equally diverse. Even in a specialty career field such as counseling, there are different levels of positions.

Career professionals generally speak of three categories of jobs for those seeking employment. Richard Nelson Bolles (2007) addressed a variation of the three job types in his seminal text *What Color Is Your Parachute?* The three categories are outlined here:

1. *The survival job.* A survival job is one a person accepts just to survive (i.e., feed and house him- or herself and his or her family). Typical survival jobs include working at fast-food restaurants, waiting tables, taking graveyard shifts as a custodian, clerking in a department store, making telemarketing calls, and many more. Survival jobs simply allow the counseling graduate student or professional to exist while his or her professional job search continues. It's likely many counselors reading this text have had several survival-type jobs. (Shannon had almost 20 different survival jobs from his freshman year until he earned his doctorate.)

2. *Intermediate job.* An intermediate job is just what you would assume: employment somewhere in between what you have already accomplished and your desired career goal. Intermediate jobs are the professional way station on the road to your life's work. Unlike survival jobs, intermediate jobs for counselors are related to the counseling field and may, in fact, be actual counseling jobs. For counseling professionals, examples of intermediate jobs include case manager, bachelor's-level addictions counselor, or a beginning counseling position in a less prestigious agency, school, or college. Counselors and other professionals accept intermediate jobs to gain experience in the field or as a stepping stone for future advancement. We know of one counselor who, having completed his doctorate in counselor

education but unable to land his dream job in college counseling, accepted a position as a clinical director of a county clinic in an underserved region in the western United States.

3. *Dream job.* The dream job is what all counselor educators and counselors covet, an opportunity to self-actualize, in counselor-speak, and it differs for everyone. Your dream-job criteria may include a number of elements: the type of position; desired geographic area; particular school, agency, or college; a supervisory role; running your own counseling practice; managing others; serving as a department chair; earning tenure as a professor; earning a healthy salary and benefits, and so forth. Regardless of where you are in your job search, the dream job is the brass ring on the carousel.

Obtaining your dream job usually is the culmination of many years—if not decades—of education, related work, sacrifice, and careful planning and is often preceded by much struggle and disappointment.

A Few Points About These Categories

One counselor's intermediate job could be another's dream job. It's all very subjective, based on your own personal values. Remember the colleague who became a clinical director of an isolated county clinic? He considered this a stepping stone to his long-term goal. Another counselor might look at this as a dream opportunity to improve the lives of those living in a small community.

Sometimes dream opportunities grow out of intermediate or even survival jobs. If you are deliberate in the types of survival jobs you take and cognizant of the skills that you are developing along the way, you can effectively prepare for and create dream opportunities.

Now that you have been formally introduced (or, more appropriately, *reminded*) of the three categories of jobs, let's spend a little time addressing how to successfully negotiate them.

Finding Great Survival Jobs

You may already have successfully transitioned to the intermediate level of job search, but if you are just completing a master's degree in one of the various counseling programs, you still may be working in a survival job.

Survival jobs don't have to be drudgery. Your outlook and enthusiasm for your work can provide many opportunities for skill development that will serve you well as you proceed to the intermediate and dream-job levels of employment.

Because counseling is governed by a strong ethical code shared by all practitioners, opportunities to observe or "job shadow" really don't exist. You can learn a lot about the field, though, by taking administrative jobs with organizations that provide counseling services. Understanding the business operations of a counseling center—including managing budgets, filing insurance papers, and maintaining confidentiality—develop long-term skills that may prove beneficial in the long run.

If you identify your dream job, then you can target survival and intermediate jobs that will help you to develop the skills and knowledge base necessary to fulfill the responsibilities of that dream job and to effectively market yourself for that position when you've adequately prepared for it.

Marketing Tools

As you pursue employment, you may want to use a number of marketing tools in your job search. Here are descriptions of some of the most helpful tools and suggested uses for each:

- *Curriculum vitae (also known as a CV or vita).* This is a detailed accounting of one's professional life, including courses, workshops, and presentations that have been taught; published works (books, manuscripts, and articles); employment; licensure; certification; community service; professional manuscripts; and honors and awards. This document is most commonly used when applying for positions in educational or research institutions or for grant applications or an award related to academic or research entities. In those cases in which the included information is voluminous, it is often accompanied by an executive summary. CV's are most commonly used in higher education.
- *Résumé.* Although a résumé often shares many of the same elements and uses as a CV, the most effective résumés are best developed as brief documents, specifically addressing experiences and highlighting accomplishments that are most closely aligned with a specific type of position. Individuals with broad experiences may have several versions of their résumé, targeting a variety of applications of their backgrounds.
- *Executive summary.* Up to (but not exceeding) a page in length, the executive summary is most often presented as a synopsis of one's professional experiences that are most closely aligned with the activity for which the document has been prepared. When accompanying a CV, the executive summary takes on many properties of a résumé, highlighting accomplishments and targeting specific activities related to the submission. In a résumé, the executive summary serves as an overview of the remainder of the document and, when well devised, encourages the reader to seek additional information.
- *Bio.* The bio is similar to the executive summary in its brevity, but it is meant to be read, not scanned. It addresses a need for information about your background without boring the reader with the minutiae of your career path. The bio includes basic biographical information (name, educational background, etc.), scope of practice, career highlights, and contact information. This is the document that humanizes you, so you may want to include some information about family, hobbies, or community activities. In these days of identity theft and other crimes, though, please be careful when sharing personal information. (If you need an example of how a bio should read, pick up almost any published book with scholarly or self-help overtones and examine the "About the Author" entry.)

These four documents (CV, résumé, executive summary, and bio) should be updated on a regular basis (at least once a year but more effectively once a quarter), so they are available when opportunity knocks. Any one of them is appropriately accompanied by a

- *Cover letter.* As its name suggests, this is the letter that "covers" your résumé or CV. The best (and most effective) cover letters are brief and specifically prepared for the opportunity and should accomplish three things: (a) present concise reasoning as to why you are a strong candidate for the position or award for which you are applying; (b) share enough of your background to create interest to encourage the reader to look at your résumé; and (c) provide an opportunity for follow-up regarding your candidacy. This is not the place for a lengthy "philosophy of counseling" statement. (That is best handled as a separate document presented as an appendix to your CV or résumé.) If your cover letter exceeds three to four paragraphs and one typewritten page, it's time to edit.

Here are a few other recommendations for your marketing arsenal:

- *Press releases.* Present a free seminar in conjunction with a community organization and promote it through the local news media. In addition to newspaper and television entities, don't forget school newsletters, library information boards, grocery store community boards, and church bulletins. Name recognition is the goal here.
- *Web sites.* In the age of the Internet, a Web site legitimizes your business. Especially for those pursuing private practice, an Internet presence is rapidly becoming a necessity. Make certain your Web site contains the appropriate buzz words that will be captured by search engines.
- *Business cards.* In your word-of-mouth marketing plan, there is no easier leave-behind than a business card. Besides providing contact information, the flip side of the card can be used to list services provided to clients.
- *Brochures.* Think of a brochure as a business card on steroids with a bio attached. These can be instrumental marketing tools for practices that actively seek referrals through auxiliary entities: Provide bundles to your contacts and let them share the information.

Recognizing Resources for Your Job Search

If you are in the process of completing a degree, you're already on the path to the next level of employment because the most effective strategy for moving up the career ladder is to earn a master's degree (or doctorate) and to begin contacting potential employers about professional counseling positions. There are several methods you can use to identify and secure appropriate positions. A savvy job seeker will understand and pursue all appropriate methods.

Your University Career Center

A good first stop on the way to gainful employment can be found at your own university, specifically, the campus career center. Although services provided vary from campus to campus, at a minimum this is a place to find assistance with résumé and CV development, job search correspondence, employer research, and interviewing skills. Many campuses allow those entering the job market to review their own interview performance by means of videotaped interviews, usually under the guidance of a career counselor or a "guest employer," as a way to improve their skills in this area. (Until you've actually seen yourself on tape, you may not be aware of fidgeting, nervous gesturing, and verbal pausing—*uhs, you knows, I means,* and *likes.*)

Professionals at your campus career center can be instrumental in helping you to prepare for your job search. These professionals can function as a second set of eyes for your résumé or CV, a critic for your cover letters and interview skills, and an advisor for using resources both inside and outside of the career services office.

Some types of jobs are more likely than others to be promoted through university career centers. For school counseling positions, especially, employers use a much more formalized hiring process, so many recruiters will participate in campus job fairs and recruit through connections in the campus career center. Registration for services through the campus career center is almost always a requirement to participate in these programs.

Traditional Job Search Resources

Most human services agencies do not actively recruit in the same fashion as school districts. The traditional approach, then, to securing jobs in this type of environment is to read and respond to ads in the newspaper and other print media.

The Internet has also gained popularity as a job search resource, and several online job boards have become excellent resources for job advertisements.

Here is a list of some of the best places to find counseling jobs advertised:

- *Counseling Today,* a monthly magazine published by the American Counseling Association (ACA) and included in the cost of membership (*Counseling Today* is particularly useful for university teaching and college counseling positions)
- The ACA Web site (www.counseling.org; from the home page, select "Career Center," then choose the JobCenter option)
- Newsletters and Web sites for the many ACA divisions
- The *Chronicle of Higher Education,* which also has on online edition (again, best for university positions; the Web site allows you to set up a job alert, e-mailing you when positions meeting your specifications are posted), which also has an online edition, www.chroniclecareers. com (for humorous advice regarding faculty career and workplace matters, click on the Ms. Mentor section of the Web site) and offers a blog at www.Chronicle.com/onhiring
- www.CareerBuilder.com

- www.Indeed.com (this Web site compiles advertisements from all of the other major sites; you can set up a job alert to send you a daily listing of all positions meeting the criteria you set)

Technological advances come at such lightning speed that any list of Web sites provided here will change by the time it is published. A great way to find resources is to use an Internet search engine. A keyword search such as "counseling jobs nonprofit Ohio" (or a similar search that defines your criteria) should produce a list that you can peruse for great opportunities.

Using your university's career center and identifying job opportunities in the newspaper and on the Internet are only two job search approaches, and although some counselors do get jobs this way, Bolles (2007) encourages job seekers to tap into the "hidden job market."

Hidden Job Market

The hidden job market is one in which positions have not been advertised. Estimates of how many people are employed through the hidden job market range upward from 65% of all new hires (Bolles, 2004). When you understand the investment (or the costs) of hiring a single new employee, you will begin to find ways to make the process more cost-effective for potential employers. That is the secret to tapping into the hidden job market.

Organizations do not advertise opportunities for a number of reasons, but the one that tops the list, particularly for nonprofit entities, is budget. Let's review some of the potential costs involved in hiring a new employee:

- *Advertising a position opening.* Depending on the length of the advertisement, the length of the run, and the number of papers or other media outlets, advertising can cost hundreds, or even thousands, of dollars.
- *Responding to applicants.* If you are an employer who has placed an advertisement, you may have upward of 100 applicants for any given position. Simply sending a one-page letter in an envelope involves the costs of paper, envelopes, ink cartridges, and postage, plus the cost of the labor involved in writing, printing, folding, collating, stamping, and sending the letter. Even if you respond via e-mail, you still have the personnel costs of setting up the database, composing the letter, proofing a mail merge, and following up on bounced messages. (This is one reason applicants do not always receive a reply from employing organizations.)
- *Interview costs.* Many organizations pay for candidates' travel costs outright or reimburse candidates for them. This may include air fare, parking, hotel stays, meals, and so forth.
- *Opportunity costs.* For important hiring decisions, a number of people may be consulted in the interviewing process. When key personnel are involved in meeting potential new employees, they aren't able to participate in other (often revenue-producing) activities.
- *Training costs.* Training new employees can reduce the productivity of current staff members, which is also an opportunity cost. Sending

new employees to special training seminars involves registration, travel, and other related costs.

- *Accommodation costs.* Employees need a place to work, appropriate furnishings, communication devices (phone, computer, etc.), lighting, office supplies and equipment, a nameplate for their desk, business cards, stationery, and so forth.
- *Psychic costs.* The investment of time and energy in identifying personnel can be enormous.

If a potential employer could avoid many of these costs, wouldn't it make sense for him or her to do so? As a job seeker, how you creatively address some of these costs gives you an opportunity to get the proverbial foot in the door and make a positive and lasting impression on a hiring authority.

Networking

Networking is the single most effective way to tap into the hidden job market because it is inherently a multitasking function. Many great networking opportunities occur when key staff members are already involved in professional development or training activities: attending meetings, participating in seminars or conferences, or experiencing downtime during these activities.

Counselors are natural networkers. Simply having a conversation with other people about the work they do is the basis of good networking. Listening for opportunities and following up with key information are additional elements of good networking skills. One of the new, high-tech methods of networking is LinkedIn (www.linkedin.com), a Web site through which small business owners, counselors, consultants, and anyone else can network across the globe through the miracle of technology. Many of you reading this text likely already are part of LinkedIn or another social networking Web site.

One example of specific networking in the job search process is known as *informational interviewing*. In its purest form, an informational interview is set up by an individual who wants to learn more about a specific career or organization. He or she will contact a practicing professional to request time to ask questions about what the professional does, what his or her organization does, and what steps he or she took to get there.

One of Shannon's students had this experience with informational interviewing:

One of my students called an addictions treatment agency to inquire about the type of training necessary to be hired as an addictions counselor. After some persistence (she had to call back three times), she secured an appointment with an assistant manager. The student and manager made a good connection at the meeting, and the manager asked her to leave a résumé, which she did. (*Note: Always take a résumé to an informational interview!*)

Four months later, he called to tell her they would soon have an opening and wanted to know whether she was still interested. You bet she was!

Because she made a prior positive connection, she was at the top of the list and was hired.

Remember, when an agency or school gets a pile of applications, you want yours to be on the top. The informational interview turns applicants into known entities who are more likely to be highly ranked as the list of candidates is shortened.

Internships and Practicums

In the grand scheme of the job search, internship and practicum sites rank among the most effective elements of a great networking strategy. Although not every counselor attains employment at the school or agency where they have interned, some will. More important, the practicum and internship provide a critical step in establishing credentials for the beginning counselor, but beyond the professional practice skills these counselors earn are the relationships they build with supervisors and other professional staff members. Tapping into the networks of these established professionals will often yield the best job leads. A strong recommendation by a professional counselor in the field is often preferred over that of a counselor educator because the field supervisor has been in a position to observe the student's work with real clients.

Faculty Positions in Counselor Education

Counseling professionals who are seeking a faculty position will as a minimal requirement need a doctorate in counselor education. To build on this foundation, good mentoring by faculty in your doctoral program is crucial. Our experience, however, has been that some counselor education doctoral students feel they did not receive adequate mentoring in their doctoral program. So, academic wannabes, pay heed to these suggestions! Besides the doctorate and research capability, teaching experience is certainly very important, especially for counselor education programs that offer only terminal master's degrees in counseling. Master's-degree-only programs will usually put more—or at least as much— emphasis on teaching expertise as on research ability. Thus, get as much teaching experience as possible as a doctoral student or as an adjunct after completing your doctorate. The real litmus test for faculty is your ability to publish in academic journals. In many doctoral programs, students routinely publish articles with the faculty through the mentoring process we mentioned earlier. Those who don't may wish to seek out the advice of their advisor or major professor about specific journals. Generally, publishing in state journals or national newsletters is a more realistic goal for students who have never submitted an academic article.

Publish or Perish

Publications vary within the vast academic fields that make up higher education. In the humanities, books are considered the top shelf of publications. In fields such as counseling and psychology, academic journals are actually considered above books, especially flagship journals (e.g., *Journal of Counseling & Development*). Books are very important, but they are more important when the author has publications in academic, referred journals and when the publisher is known in the field.

Again, two critical areas on which aspiring faculty must focus are publications and teaching experience. Most counselor education faculty positions will lean more on your publications. An additional factor for doctoral students and future faculty or assistant professors is to get on editorial boards of scholarly journals. Although flagship journals such as the *Journal of Counseling & Development* will seek more established scholars, divisional and state journals may be open to doctoral students and newly minted PhDs. As a member of a journal's editorial review board, you will learn the submission and critique process firsthand. Editorial review boards provide good experience and will facilitate your developing an aesthetic for what is good technical writing and what isn't. We also recommend that you consider the merit of becoming an ad hoc reviewer to gain valuable experience with academic journals.

Other important factors for counselor educators in the job search market are memberships in professional associations such as ACA and its affiliates. Most significantly, the Association of Counselor Education and Supervision is a must membership for aspiring professors. If you are applying for a position as a professor of school counseling, you should be a member of the American School Counselor Association (ASCA). If you are seeking an academic position in mental health counseling, you should be a member of the American Mental Health Counselors Association (AMHCA), and so forth. Professional presentations at conferences are important as well, and most doctoral students have likely presented at a state, regional, or national conference.

The Visioning Process: Creating Your Dream

Career search professionals will tell you that the first order of success is the ability to visualize a desired goal. The second, and more important, task is to create a strategy for achieving the goal. One of the most common methods being taught in career classes, among marketing professionals, and in professional coaching networks is creative visualization, or "visioning" for short.

Visioning is a simple concept arising from the work of John Holland, Richard Nelson Bolles, and many other education, career field, business, and spiritual leaders. Notable leaders with a determined vision (or visionaries) are Gandhi, Martin Luther King Jr., Mother Teresa, the current Dalai Lama, and many others. A counselor need not be a famous leader to create a vision for his or her life and career, however. Visioning is the easier, creative part of crafting your counseling career. You just need to follow some basic steps. We recommend that you consider this visioning process before you launch your job search:

- *Personal history.* How did you get where you are? What experiences led you down the road to becoming a counselor or counselor educator? How does your personal history influence you as a counselor?
- *Values.* Psychologist Milton Rokeach (2000) did pioneering work in the study of values. Rokeach's work suggests that successful people find work congruent with their personal values. More mature counselors may understand their values better because they are more con-

crete. Regardless of age, consider how your values might affect your search and career. For example, if being close to family is an important consideration, you will be limited to a particular geographical area. If a school counselor desires work in a church-affiliated school, such values should be foremost in his or her mind during a job search.

- *Professional identity.* This step would seem to be a no brainer because the reader is surely a counselor of some type. However, given that working professionals in the United States will likely have at least three careers in their lifetime rather than one (Bolles, 2004), identity is more complex than it appears. For example, we know of one rehabilitation counselor who decided in middle age that he wanted to work in a public school setting and returned to graduate school to achieve that, transforming his identity considerably. Shannon had considerable struggles to discern whether he would become a dean of students, director of a university counseling center, or a counselor educator. Over time, he has been all three. Many of you reading this text will move from being a counselor to being a clinical supervisor; administrator of a school, clinic, or human services agency; or perhaps dean of a college.

- *Goal.* What is your ultimate professional goal? Running a school counseling office? Becoming department chair of a large counselor education program? Opening a pastoral counseling center serving the emotional and spiritual needs of low-income people? Does being dean of students at a small college interest you? To achieve your goal, you must first understand what it is. Certainly, goals are fluid and open to occasional revision, but successful people set clear goals and regularly check their progress in achieving them (Covey, 1996).

- *Action plan.* Everyone with a vision needs a plan to achieve it. An action plan is a road map to success and should consist of concrete steps leading up to the vision. For example, if your vision is to become president of the ASCA, your action plan needs several ascending steps and might look something like this:

1. Becoming active in the local school counseling organization (1–3 years)
2. Transitioning into a state leadership role (1–4 years)
   a. Helping to plan the state conference
   b. Serving on the state journal's editorial board
   c. Being elected as vice president or president
3. Serving a leadership role in an affiliated regional organization (2 years)
4. Writing articles for an ASCA journal or the national newsletter (ongoing)
5. Volunteering at ACA and ASCA annual conventions where you continue networking to get to know national leaders (2–4 years)
6. Volunteering and being selected for national committees (2–4 years)

7. Running and eventually being elected to a national leadership position (2–4 years)
8. Running for ASCA president—and losing
9. Running again for ASCA president: *You win!*

- *Time frame.* Anywhere from 8 to 10 years, perhaps more or, in some cases, less. Remember: You may need to revise your action plan because of changes, setbacks, moves, job changes, family considerations, and so forth. Our point here is that achieving a lofty vision may take years.
- *Review.* You need to regularly check on your progress toward your vision to gauge how you are progressing. Does your vision need to be amended or timelines reconsidered? Have your values changed over time?

Techniques Used in Career Visioning

- *Visioning (or what some call "dreaming").* A critical component of this phase is asking "What do I want in my career?" and "How can I create what I want in my career?" Successful people from all fields visualize what they want, then take steps to make it a reality (Capacchione, 2000).
- *Meditation.* This phase assists you in discerning the creative self that lies within you. Many ideas come from this silent phase.
- *Visualization.* What do you seek from your career? Regarding your career, where would you want to be in 5 to 7 years? A clinical director? Director of a school counseling program? A tenured counselor education professor? Running your own private practice?
- *Focusing.* This phase helps you to clarify how to plan and prioritize the preceding visualization process. For example, what needs to happen before you can open your own private practice or run a school counseling program?
- *Creative journaling.* The journaling process allows you to document how your job search–visioning process is going. There will be successes and disappointments along the way. When you receive a job offer (or achieve something desirable, e.g., being elected president of your local counseling organization), record what this success means to you. Likewise, record what each failure means. Remember, failure isn't always failing. Sometimes we succeed later only because we fail initially (Hodges, 2001).
- *Collage making.* Don't denigrate this potentially creative, concrete exercise. A career collage helps you create a tangible picture of your career dream.
- *Interviewing.* Choose two or three people whom you respect (and who are willing to provide honest feedback that some friends and family will not). Ask them to answer these four questions either in writing or verbally:

1. What qualities does this person (you) possess that will help make her (him) successful in his (her) career quest?
2. What steps does this person need to take to realize her (his) career goal(s)?
3. This person's strongest quality is _____.
4. This person's chief weakness appears to be _____.

Once you have determined what your career dreams include, it becomes much easier to evaluate whether advertised positions fit in with your career goals. You may see many positions for which you are qualified, but because you have identified your long-term goals, you will be able to recognize that these positions do little to develop the skill sets you would require to advance to your dream job.

In this vein, you may recognize a great opportunity to reach your long-term goals that comes with a short-term hardship. Many a professional has taken a short-term position to "get a card punched" to move on to loftier goals.

Should I Apply for Jobs in Geographic Areas That Don't Appeal to Me?

Because modern society is much more mobile than in decades past, counselors and counselor educators may be faced with the difficult decision of applying for and accepting a job far away from their family, friends, and roots. For many, applying for jobs in distant states (or even countries) can be exciting, but for others, especially counselors with close family ties, contemplating moving a far distance can be traumatic. It is also safe to say that most counselors have in mind in what section of the country they wish to reside and work. Unfortunately, many counselors will be faced with sacrificing a preferred region, state, or city because of greater opportunity elsewhere. In this section, we offer several suggestions regarding moving to a geographical area that may not be your first choice.

There are numerous issues to consider when entering the job market. One of the most significant is whether to relocate. Because of economic concerns, many of today's counselors and counselor educators will be required to move to a different area, state, or region, and perhaps even overseas. In the area in which Shannon most recently lived, graduates in school counseling are almost compelled to apply for out-of-state jobs because of market saturation in the area. Thus, many graduates of his university's school counseling program accept jobs in Virginia, North and South Carolina, Florida, Texas, and Arizona. The South and the Sun Belt offer the most opportunities, although they can also mean high costs of living. The case for relocation can certainly be made for those seeking a counselor education faculty position. No one can make the decision for you, but we offer some issues for consideration:

Split the page in half by drawing a line down the middle. Label one section *Pros* and the other section *Cons*.

Should I take the job in Los Angeles?

Pros	Cons
It's a job	A large, urban area
Good pay and benefits	Expensive area
Diverse community and school	Overcrowded schools
Warm weather	Earthquakes and water shortages
Spouse or partner has opportunities	Spouse or partner may have opportunities elsewhere
I will likely have other offers.	

In many cases, the individual making the Pro–Con list discovers that the pros significantly outnumber the cons or vice versa. In the preceding list, the pros and cons seem pretty equal, leaving the counselor with a difficult decision to make. If you are in a marriage or partnership, certainly you will need to make such a decision jointly. Given that the U.S. Department of Labor (2008) has maintained that counseling is a field that should grow faster than average for the foreseeable future, counselors, unlike those in some professional fields, can likely find other jobs in areas more conducive to their interests.

Counselor educators seeking faculty positions will have less freedom than school and agency counselors. To break into the field and obtain a faculty position, you may have to accept one in a less desirable area. After you have established yourself as a professor and scholar, you will gain more mobility.

Demystifying
the Job Search Process

In this chapter, we attempt to remove the mystery shrouding the process of how counselors are actually hired.

We know that beginning your first job search can be a bit daunting. Don't be discouraged! Remind yourself that there are thousands of people who have successfully navigated this obstacle course and are now gainfully employed in the counseling field. You will likely become one of them, and when this phase is all over, you may shake your head in awe and wonder at the complexity of the process.

Begin with the premise that many organizations that hire counselors may not have an *individual* who serves in a personnel function, let alone an *entire human resources department* to coordinate hiring. Consider that organizations advertising a position are probably already short staffed, so they are eager to identify and hire a qualified candidate as quickly as possible. Further consider that the individual or individuals tasked with the responsibility of identifying a qualified candidate may already have administrative, publication, and client service responsibilities.

So, onto a plate that is already full, we are now heaping pages and pages of cover letters, résumés, and curricula vitae (CVs) that must be reviewed, winnowed, and appropriately pursued. (In larger organizations, add a search committee and an Equal Employment Opportunity Commission officer who must coordinate staff and candidate schedules, and you'll understand why some searches may take *months* to complete!)

As much as you, the candidate, would like to believe that the potential employer or search chair absorbs every single word of your 50-page CV, you need to recognize that at least in the initial review stage, this just isn't going to happen. Some experts have estimated that 30 seconds is the average time for an initial review of application materials. Others argue that this is a generous estimate. Your application packet has—*possibly*—10 to 30 seconds to present your case for inclusion in the pile that will be considered further.

Assume that your credentials are competing with those of 200 other applicants—not an unlikely number for an advertised position. Any résumé that is shoddily prepared or accompanied by a cover letter with spelling and grammatical errors will not make the cut. Next to go are those candidates who have not demonstrated that they meet the minimum qualifications set forth for the position.

From here on, the process becomes more subjective. For our purposes, let's continue with this possible scenario:

Three piles are created during the initial review: Great Candidates! Meets Qualifications, and Send a Nice Thank You Letter (SANTYL). The SANTYL pile is history. If there are enough Great Candidates, the Meets Qualifications will join the SANTYLs in receiving a "thank you for playing" note (assuming there's a budget for this).

So, now that the wheat has been separated from the chaff, the process of ranking the Great Candidates ensues. Three to 5 top candidates, with a ranked-second pool to round out the top 10 (allowing for the possibility that some of the Great Candidates may have already received and accepted a job offer), will advance to the next stage, in this case a telephone interview.

From there, on-site interviews, followed by reference checks of the top candidate, then extension of an offer, all of which are much more complicated than a single sentence can adequately describe, complete the cycle.

Sadly, but predictably, some candidates who really *were* Great Candidates weren't identified as such and thereby didn't make the cut.

Some candidates otherwise labeled as minimally qualified may, however, have been bumped up to the next tier by a well-written cover letter that clearly delineated their qualifications, making the reviewer's job easier. Still others may have earned a second review of their credentials by placing a well-timed phone call and asking questions about the position and the selection process, establishing rapport with the search chair. And remember in the last chapter when we discussed networking? This is how a candidate not previously being considered might be added to the mix.

Subsequent chapters have more information about résumés and cover letters, but for now, we're focusing on the mechanism of hiring candidates because understanding the process will provide you, the job seeker, with foundational information that will help you to avoid missteps that could eliminate you from consideration.

In subsequent sections, we introduce you to concepts and share personal experiences designed to illuminate and educate you.

Search Committee

Regardless of whether you're seeking a counseling position in a middle school, county agency, or community college or as a counselor educator in a graduate program, you will be addressing a search committee. You may already have served on such a committee as a teacher, agency counselor, or graduate student.

As veterans of numerous search committees in higher education and community agencies, our experience dictates that all search committees are similar and, at the same time, different.

- Search committees in *counselor education*, for example, involve a broad array of campus officials—academic administrators such as deans, librarians, graduate students, and faculty from a variety of disciplines, including, of course, counselor education.
- Search committees in *college and community college counseling* may include representatives from academic affairs, student affairs, and students in addition to counseling professionals.
- Search committees in *school counseling* may well consist of teachers and administrators as well as counselors.
- Search committees for *community agencies* will be made up of mental health professionals, social workers, counselors, and so forth.

Regardless of the type of school, college, or agency, all search committees have at least two common purposes: to solicit and select the "best" candidate and to conduct a "perfect" search process.

The first and most important bit of information to remember about search committees is that despite their best efforts, they are imperfect and apt to make mistakes. Now, this statement is scarcely earth shattering, but our experience has been that candidates we have counseled are frequently shocked at being rejected.

"It just didn't make sense," one disappointed applicant said to me. "I mean, they chose someone straight out of graduate school over an experienced school counselor like me."

This applicant, who was indeed a very strong candidate, could not reconcile that he had not been selected, based on the stated job description. This very example, though, illustrates an imperative all applicants must learn: Job searches and selections do not necessarily have to make sense. By this statement we do not mean to imply that they are whimsical and arbitrary. In fact, given that many highly educated people on search committees are sifting through applications and conducting interviews, most are pretty thorough. But what "makes sense" to the applicant, who usually does not have access to inside information, may be perfectly rational to the selection committee.

Here's an example of search committee decision making:

Several years ago, I served on a search committee charged with filling a senior-level student affairs position. An ad placed in the venerable *Chronicle of Higher Education* netted upward of 60 applications.

After the screening process, during which committee members ranked the candidates on a 1–5 scale for experience, degree, letters of recommendation, and the like, the pool was whittled down to some 20 applications, then down to 10, whom we interviewed by phone. From that number, 5 candidates were invited for on-campus interviews.

Then the process got interesting.

After the interviews were completed, the search committee came together with their rankings. The members of the search committee (who numbered just under 10) had such disparate rankings that the task of selecting a candidate seemed implausible. (It was reminiscent of that black-and-white film classic *Twelve Angry Men*, although missing the finesse of Henry Fonda and certainly resulting in less dire consequences.)

During the decision-making process, the biases and priorities really emerged: A faculty member wanted an administrator who had been an academic, one of the administrators wanted someone with a business background because the position involved major budgetary responsibilities, one member wanted to hire his friend, and the students preferred the most charismatic candidate.

Our charge was to rank order the candidates for the vice provost so she could make the final decision. Unfortunately, given the skewed rankings of the committee members, this proved impossible. The committee chair tabulated the individual members' votes per candidate, wrote a narrative of the process, and passed the information along to the vice provost. The vice provost took what seemed an inordinate amount of time and then selected the candidate whom almost everyone on the committee agreed was the weakest. (I do not intend to imply this candidate was not qualified, but rather that all search committee members thought he seemed less well qualified than his competition.)

Although no one was certain why the vice provost selected this candidate, he was hired. The only thing we on the search committee could figure was that the successful candidate was the one who drew the least criticism.

Now, this particular experience is not the norm, but it does illustrate that the selection process can seem puzzling, even to those who are active participants. Although a candidate cannot control the outcome of a search, she or he must do everything to ensure his or her candidacy is as competitive as possible.

We offer our own thoughts and suggestions, based on decades of serving on search committees, preparing to face search committees, and coaching candidates to prepare for the search process and our own successes and failures with search committees.

Looking for Counselor Education Positions

Search committees in higher education tend to be more complex, larger, and more diverse than those in most K–12 schools and in community agencies. The very nature of counselor education provides a framework in which one prepares for the cutting edge of a global, multicultural profession. Counseling has expanded overseas, and organizations such as the International Association for Counselling (ICA) offer a glimpse of the profession's future (Arthur & Pedersen, 2008). Thus, when preparing to search for a position in counselor education, it is imperative that you understand and be able to articulate what psychologist Daniel Goleman (1995) calls *cultural EQ* (Emotional Quotient). Also, you must understand you are entering what is rapidly becoming a diverse, global, dynamic profession.

Most counselor education faculty positions are advertised in the *Chronicle of Higher Education* and in *Counseling Today*. Although academic positions may also be advertised in regional, state, and local newspapers, these resources offer the widest and broadest dissemination of information, ensuring for hiring authorities a national (or international) search that reaches a diverse candidate pool.

The *Chronicle* is published in both a traditional newspaper format and also an online version. The *Chronicle* lists classified ads in alphabetical order by field. Display ads are more prominent and are often used to advertise higher level opportunities or multiple positions at the same institution. The print version of the publication has an index to current listings in the front of its Careers section, which is very helpful in locating positions within the paper. You can also set up an online alert (go to www.thechronicle.com) to be notified via e-mail whenever any position meeting your specifications is posted. If you prefer looking through the newspaper, your university library probably has a subscription to the *Chronicle*, and you can also subscribe yourself. The articles are often quite interesting and provide an overview of the philosophy and business of higher education.

The other viable resource for counselor education positions is *Counseling Today*, the monthly magazine published by the American Counseling Association (ACA). *Counseling Today* ads are also listed online on the Career Center page of the ACA Web site, www.counseling.org. Several of ACA's divisions also provide position listings through their newsletters and Web sites.

Additional publications to consult are the *Affirmative Action Registry*, newspapers in large cities, and Web sites of individual colleges and universities.

Resources and Other Things You Should Know

In targeting a career in counselor education, you need to be prepared to demonstrate that you are an applicant with strong connections to the profession. A membership in the ACA is an absolute must, as is a membership in the ACA division representing your area of interest. For school counselors, that would be the American School Counselor Association (ASCA); for mental health counselors, the American Mental Health Counselors Association (AMHCA) would be the association of choice, and family counselors are most identified with the International Association of Marriage and Family Counselors (IAMFC). Aspiring counselor education faculty will find that the Association for Counselor Education and Supervision (ACES) most closely fits their professional goals. ACES, which represents counselor education and supervision concerns, is the division primarily concerned with the academic training and preparation of future counselors.

Counselor educators must carefully craft their CV to highlight their education, publications, and professional presentations. Because academic reputations are built on research, publications are your most significant form of portable wealth (Gray & Drew, 2008). Also, serving on journal editorial boards is very helpful in terms of securing employment. If you are a graduate student, state association journals are a good place to begin.

When applying for a faculty position in counselor education, make sure you have updated your CV (see our suggestions in chap. 3), have a research presentation you can make—preferably in PowerPoint—and verify that your references will write outstanding letters of recommendation for you. A lukewarm letter of recommendation is not likely to provide much support for your candidacy. You also need to carefully prepare and practice for the interview. Interviewing is covered in more detail in chapter 4.

Searching for a College or University Counseling Center Position

College and university counseling centers, although still dominated by the psychology profession, employ many counselors. Small colleges (5,000 full-time equivalents or fewer) are more likely to hire master's-level counselors than are large universities, and the cost-effectiveness of hiring at this level makes these institutions more likely to advertise for master's-level counselors and social workers.

Careers in college counseling should be planned carefully. Master's-level counselors would be wise to serve an internship in a college counseling center if they are interested in a career in college counseling. Directors of college counseling prefer professionals who have some experience and a working knowledge of college counseling, although this is not always the case. College counseling centers are most often separate entities from career centers or student health centers. In the age of fiscal accountability, however, counseling is frequently combined with career services, health services, and occasionally academic advising. Thus, previous experience in career services or student health is advantageous when searching for college counseling positions. College counseling centers still receive many, if not most, of their referrals from residence advisors, so a background in university housing (or college student personnel administration) can be helpful as well.

Besides a background in college counseling, residence life, academic advising, and so forth, we recommend that you join the American College Counseling Association (ACCA). ACCA has some 2,000 members and offers an electronic mailing list, Web site (www.collegecounseling.org/), a popular journal (the *Journal of College Counseling*), and a convention every 2 years. Additional resources to be aware of are Archer and Cooper (1998), Davis and Humphrey (2000), Kadison and DiGeronimo (2004), Lippincott and Lippincott (2007), and Singaravelu and Pope (2007). Perusing back issues of the *Journal of College Counseling* for background information related to college student mental health is also a helpful strategy. In the era of high-profile tragedies at Virginia Tech, Northern Illinois University, and others, a thorough understanding of psychiatric issues, and crisis and trauma training and experience, will enhance basic counseling credentials and strengthen your candidacy for these types of opportunities.

Where to Search

As with counselor education faculty positions, there are several vehicles to use when conducting your search. The *Chronicle of Higher Education* is the publication of choice for most college counseling positions. As previously noted, checking the printed copy or the online version (www.thechronicle.com) weekly is helpful. ACCA's electronic mailing list is another means through which jobs are posted, although you must be a member to have access. Previously, the American College Personnel Association (ACPA) national convention was a screening location for college counselors, but because the profession has moved away from ACPA, no current national gathering offers comprehensive screening for college counseling positions.

The Reality

Competition for college and university counseling positions is high (Lippincott & Lippincott, 2007), and any counselor planning a career therein must be willing to relocate. Letters of recommendation from clinical supervisors in college counseling centers are crucial. Recommendations from directors of college counseling centers are particularly important because networking is conducted within the Association of University and College Counseling Center Directors (AUCCCD). It helps greatly if you apply for an opening at a center whose director knows your director. Still, Shannon's experience as a veteran and former director of a university counseling center is that such openings will generate a high number of applications. So, be prepared: Landing a college counseling position may require patience on your part. If you do not meet with initial success in landing a college position, it is possible to move from another type of counseling position, for example community mental health counseling, into college counseling. Targeting agencies that work with similar populations can provide transferrable experience and is a strategy that Shannon pursued when, unable to land a viable university position, he accepted a position in a mental health clinic. His experience working with people with severe psychopathology was instrumental as he continued to prepare for work on a college campus. University administrators, especially, have become more keenly aware of the stress that students with severe mental disorders place on their institutions (Gallagher, 2007; Kadison & DiGeronimo, 2004), so experience with populations who have conditions beyond basic adjustment issues is attractive.

Searching for a School Counseling Position

Institutions hiring for school counseling positions tend to have more centralized employment procedures than those for most other counseling positions. Many school districts actively recruit at educational fairs. A critical factor for school counselors applying for jobs is to make sure they have everything in order: a placement file, résumé, cover letter that addresses salient issues such as the ASCA National Model for school counseling (ASCA, 2009), and excellent letters of recommendation from professors and internship supervisors. In fact, the counselor who supervised such candidates on their practicum and internship likely is a more critical contact than faculty in counselor education programs because he or she has observed the student in a professional setting. Frequently, a principal or school counselor will call for a reference check to ask whether the applicant showed up to work on time, was effective in communicating with parents, and followed the school's procedures. Clearly, perspective as a member of the faculty is peripheral to such inquiries.

To Move or Not to Move

Another factor for school counselors to consider is whether relocation is a viable option. All counselors may face this, but much of the growth in school counseling is located in the Sun Belt and on the West Coast. In the Rust Belt—the upper Midwest and northeastern United States—where population demographics have been in decline, school districts have cut school counseling positions or allowed attrition to address reductions in force. Still, some recently minted school counselors are hired in these areas. In many cases, a new school counselor may take a counseling position in an inner-city school or move to another state or region, gain valuable experience for a few years, attain licensure or permanent certification (check your state's guidelines), and then return to his or her home area.

It is important to be aware of the great variation in the school counselor's functions depending on the state, particular school, and whether the position is in elementary, secondary, or high school counseling. Some schools will continue to refer to the profession as "Guidance," and others will use more current language. Elementary school counselors will do much group counseling, with some individual sessions. At the secondary level, personal and academic counseling are typically conducted by the counselor, although more frequently in conjunction with the school social worker. Most high school counselors spend by far the most significant amount of their time on academic, career, and vocational counseling, with little time left for personal counseling.

Given the realities of outcome-oriented initiatives such as the No Child Left Behind Act of 2001, the high school counselor's role is unlikely to change in the foreseeable future. The Transforming School Initiative and adoption of the American School Counselor Association (ASCA) model for school counselors will necessitate school counselors' active involvement in remediation and accountability and will change the focus to more academic and less psychological concerns. School counselors should also expect to regularly update their skill sets. In Arkansas, for example, school counselors are required to be certified to give and interpret IQ tests. Although this is unusual, a few states, especially in the South, may have a similar requirement.

We also recommend that aspiring school counselors expand their skills and tool box. Any professional planning on working in a P–12 setting should receive training in mediation, given that unresolved conflict can lead to explosive incidents and tragedies, such as those in Columbine, Colorado; Jonesboro, Arkansas; Paducah, Kentucky; and far too many areas. Also, upgrade your skills with special populations, such as those with autism spectrum disorders or attention deficit/hyperactivity disorder. You might consider seeking the advice of a veteran school counselor and getting her or his input on future trends in school counseling.

Where to Search

Students in school counseling programs should check with their career center to learn about recruitment fairs at their campus or in their area. Counselor education faculty are also good resources because faculty are often members of local school counseling organizations. (If membership is available to students—and it often is—this is an affordable and practical venue for networking.) At job fairs, you will notice that many out-of-state recruiters attend to search for counselors, teachers, psychologists, and so forth. This is your first contact, so dress as you would for an interview—because it *is* an interview! Area newspapers and school corporation or school district Web sites are also good places to look for openings.

The Reality

There are lots of school counseling positions available, but many may require relocation to a different region. If you are young and recently graduated from a school counseling program, this may prove no impediment to you. Going far away can be very exciting, but for those who have ties to a particular area, including family or community responsibilities or a partner whose career is not transferrable, moving may not be viable. If this is your situation, networking and becoming a known entity to local school corporations or districts will be your best path to employment.

Searching for a Position in Mental Health Counseling, Addictions Counseling, Rehabilitation Counseling, and Other Agency-Oriented Positions

The various agency professions in counseling—mental heath counseling, addictions counseling, rehabilitation counseling, and so forth—have a very different process for job searching than that for counselor education faculty, school counseling, and college counseling positions. Although we recognize that these are separate professions under the field's umbrella, they do share many similarities. Namely, people in these professions will counsel in inpatient and outpatient settings, not secondary schools and colleges (Remley & Herlihy, 2007). For the sake of brevity, we have listed them together here. Membership in both ACA and the ACA division representing your specialty area is recommended to enhance your professional profile. Mental health counseling professionals prefer to interview and hire applicants with a strong professional identity.

Mental health counseling represents one of the fastest growing careers in the country, with more than 100,000 mental health counselors employed in the United States (U.S. Department of Labor, 2008). This group of careers was included in *Money* magazine's "Top 50 Jobs for the Future" ("Best Jobs in America," 2006). As of 2008, 49 states; Washington, DC; and the territories of Puerto Rico and Guam licensed mental health counselors. Mental health counselors primarily work in outpatient clinics, although they also work in inpatient hospitals and residential treatment centers, college counseling, community and technical counseling centers, and many other settings (AMHCA, 2008). The U.S. Department of Labor (2008) has predicted the occupational outlook for mental health counselors to be greater than average for the foreseeable future, so if you are looking for a job in mental health, chances are very good that you will find one. There are, however, some things you need to know about searching.

Most states have adopted the Council on Accreditation for Counseling and Related Academic Programs' (CACREP's) guidelines for state licensure (Remley & Herlihy, 2007), which means a 60-semester credit program (20 classes) with a 1,000-hour practicum–internship in a mental health setting. So, if you graduated from a state that requires 48 semester credit hours, and you move to a state requiring 60 semester credit hours, you may need to complete 12 more credit hours to be license eligible. We address licensure requirements fully in chapter 8, but know this: The ability to obtain licensure will be a key factor in employment. Awareness of national standards and continuing education will be important, particularly to those counselors who anticipate frequent relocation in today's mobile society.

The hidden job market that we discussed in chapter 1 usually presents the best option for employment in a mental health agency. In many instances, agencies will hire from their internship pool. We are both aware of a number of graduating master's-level students who received job offers when their final internship was completed. Agencies that train and observe an intern for 1,000 hours usually have a good sense of the intern's skill level, work ethic, and collegial relations, so offering an available position to this known entity often makes the best fiscal sense.

Not all agencies will be able to offer all of their graduating interns a position, though. Recognize that counselors from different agencies often communicate with one another, and this can support your job search efforts. As with school and college counseling, a critical factor in employment is the on-site supervisor's evaluation of your performance. A strong evaluation could open doors to other agencies (and a mediocre or sub par evaluation will do the opposite). Communicate with your supervisor and understand what type of evaluation you are likely to receive before listing that person as a reference.

Addictions Counseling

Addictions counseling shares similarities with many other counseling jobs, but because addictions counseling does not typically require a master's degree, some significant differences in the job search process exist. Many addictions counselors are already employed in the field because they are working their way through graduate school, so an addictions counselor may have several years experience in the field by the time she or he earns the master's degree. The hiring process is very similar to that of mental health counseling, discussed earlier. Addictions counselors will also need to consider national certification and state licensure. The National Association for Alcohol and Drug Abuse Counselors (NAADC) is considered the standard in the field. Because of the difficult nature of addictions (e.g., dual diagnoses, recidivism, stress, and lower pay) addictions jobs are readily available, and counselors with addictions experience have an excellent chance at employment.

Rehabilitation Counseling

Like mental health counselors, rehabilitation counselors work in a number of settings, including agencies, hospitals, public and private agencies, and private practice (American Rehabilitation Counseling Association, 2009). Similar to mental health counselors, rehabilitation counselors work an extended internship in a clinical setting and often get their first counseling jobs through internships.

Where to Search

A job search for a mental health counseling position is more decentralized than that for counselor education, college counseling, or school counseling positions. Mental health counseling does not have a national, flagship publication in which to advertise positions, nor do people hiring mental health counselors actively recruit at job fairs in the manner of school districts. Thus, you will need to check the classified section of newspapers in areas in which you would like to apply. With rare exception, newspapers will also offer an online edition, and most will allow nonsubscribers access.

An effective method of searching for these types of positions involves the use of the Internet, specifically the Web site of the Substance Abuse and Mental Health Services Administration (SAMHSA), which is a division of the U.S. Department of Health and Human Services.

Here are step-by-step instructions to use this resource: From the SAMHSA Web site (http://mentalhealth.samhsa.gov) find the Services Locator module. (At the time of this writing, it was a box with a bright orange border, a map of the United States, and a title, "Services Locator," in the top, right-hand corner of the Web page.)

Click on the map, and it will redirect you to a page titled "Mental Health Services Locator," providing a pop-up list of all U.S. states and territories. When you select a state or territory, a list of state mental health resources is generated for you to select from: lists of mental health facilities, a directory of mental health services, state resource guide, suicide prevention programs—in short, a directory of agencies and private practices that provide mental health services. This list may be sorted by city.

So, let's say you have a desire to move to Phoenix, Arizona. You can click on Arizona, choose "Phoenix," and then scroll through five pages of mental health care providers in that city. Arm yourself with a map (or knowledge of the local geography), and you can augment your list with providers in surrounding communities.

This is the beginning of a prospect list, and although it may not be comprehensive, if you combine these findings with those in the Yellow Pages, the United Way membership list, and the Chamber of Commerce directory, it's a good start for tapping into the mental health community of a specific geographic area.

The Reality

The U.S. Department of Labor (2008) has predicted that the outlook for the counseling field will be above average for the foreseeable future. Some areas will offer more job opportunities than others. The Sun Belt and West Coast are the fastest growing regions of the United States and offer excellent employment opportunities. But it's fair to say the upper Midwest and Rust Belt areas also offer opportunities for agency counselors primarily because these areas are struggling. Economically depressed areas may, ironically enough, offer real potential for mental health counselors and addictions counselors because economic shortages create more pressure and stress for people.

Special Strategies for Dual-Career Couples

Economic realities being what they are, it is not at all unusual in today's marketplace for households to rely on two incomes. For the most part, career management can be addressed effectively on an individual basis, as needed, without major upheaval in the household. Occasionally, though, circumstances arise in which both partners seek employment simultaneously. Sometimes one partner's career requires relocation to a new area for continued professional growth, resulting in career refocus for the accompanying partner. In these cases, what can you do?

- *First, take stock of your situation.* As we discussed in chapter 1, assess what you have going for you. When you're moving a household, you may want to evaluate the big picture (income and expenses, transition issues for other family members, buying and selling a home, etc.) in addition to examining career issues specific to the trailing partner (licensure portability, availability of similar jobs, etc.)
- *Lay the groundwork for starting over.* Better yet, strive always to keep a good foundation in place for job change. Updating your résumé at least once every 6 months, keeping up with continuing education opportunities, and maintaining contact with your best references are all part of an ongoing career development strategy.
- *Build your network in the new location.* Reach out to members of professional associations to which you belong. Identify practicing professionals in organizations similar to those in which you have most recently worked. Schedule informational interviews. Also, by all means reach out to your current network to ask for referrals to contacts in your new geographic area. The mobility of our society and advent of technologies have "shrunk" the continent and the world. Chances are good that someone you know will be in a position to help you make good contacts once you've arrived in your new home.
- *Consider "portable career" opportunities.* Consulting is rapidly becoming a popular extension of or replacement for traditional careers, and for a second family income, particularly when health care expenses are addressed, it can make good economic sense as well. Home-based employment, freelance work, and temporary or project assignments have become viable options, spurred on by technological advancements that support this kind of work. Distance counseling is also a newer option, although it is still in its pioneer stage, and if you pursue this option, you'll want to be fully aware of legal and ethical implications.

- *Academic couples can look in college towns.* All across the United States, you'll find areas in which institutions of higher learning are clustered together, enabling professor types to find work commutable from a central location. Be aware, too, that some institutions in more isolated areas actively seek academic couples because their expenses to relocate new hires are reduced. Many of these institutions have experienced better retention rates, reducing their costs in recruiting new faculty members.
- *Online teaching opportunities may be an option.* More and more nontraditional students are returning to school via a virtual classroom. CACREP has granted accreditation to several counseling programs that are online, and more are certain to follow.
- *Budget and be patient.* It may take awhile to land a new job, and you may have to adjust your family finances to fit your present economic situation. Use whatever downtime you might experience to refocus your other life priorities: settling into a new home, helping children adjust to schools and schedules, establishing routines, and learning about your new community. These self-care activities are important and, in the long run, may yield greater dividends for your career than rushing into a new employment situation.

Chapter

3

Building a Model Résumé and Curriculum Vitae

A résumé is the equivalent of a passport in the world of business and industry, and the curriculum vitae (CV) is its equivalent in most of academe. Like a passport, these documents provide all of the information a potential employer needs to evaluate whether you meet the minimum qualifications for the position he or she is attempting to fill. To carry this illustration further, every stop you make along your journey (career) will provide you with a stamp for this document.

Passports expire after a designated period of time, and so do résumés. Just as you want to keep your passport up to date in case an opportunity for a trip to an exotic land comes up unexpectedly, you'll want to make sure your résumé or CV is current so you are able to respond to new opportunities in a timely manner.

We've alluded to your career as being a lifelong journey. In this chapter, our goal is to help you travel effectively throughout your career by sharing effective ways of presenting your professional credentials in an appropriate format.

Another Kind of E-Ticket: The Electronic Résumé and CV

The 21st-century employment world is radically different from the one previous generations encountered. No longer do people have just one job and live in just one state or region of the country. Many may even spend at least part of their careers working in a different country (Bolles, 2004). Talk about a journey!

The proliferation of the personal computer since *Time* magazine named it 1982's "Man of the Year" ("TIME's Man of the Year," 2009) has profoundly affected the way in which people apply for jobs. Most job advertisements now point to an online application, with applicants completing the entire process via the Internet. In this era, nearly all résumés and CVs are electronic. (If computers have always been a part of your life, this advice may seem so basic as to be unworthy of mention, but because some job seekers are of an earlier generation and are not as facile with current technology, we want to make sure all readers are prepared to provide a résumé or CV via e-mail.)

Because online applications require you to cut and paste your résumé, it is vital that your résumé be formatted correctly. Just because it looks okay as a printed copy doesn't mean that you've formatted it correctly. If you are not familiar with the terms *header, footer, margin, tab, justify,* or *table,* you may want to seek assistance from someone who is well versed in using your software's formatting features.

A résumé is the standard, accepted job summary format for almost everyone seeking employment, including counselors in schools and agencies. Counselor education faculty and college counselors will generally use a CV.

Résumé or CV?

What's the difference between a résumé and a CV? And how do you know which one you should use? Let's start with simple definitions. *Webster's Dictionary* (1992) defines *résumé* as a "condensed statement, or summary," in this case a summary of your experience. *Curriculum vitae,* or *vita* for short, is Latin for "the course of one's life."

The two terms are often used interchangeably, with *résumé* more frequently used in the general population and *vita* or *CV* more often used in academic and research environments. Both types of document relate the same type of information (academic background, work history, significant accomplishments, etc.), but the presentation and the amount of information can vary substantially.

In general, a résumé is a one- to two-page (sometimes a little longer) document that concisely describes an individual's professional background. Because of the widespread use and availability of computers, the résumé has evolved over the past 20 years to become a document targeted to a specific purpose. With a few keystrokes and a good printer, a résumé can be transformed to appropriately address the advertised needs of a potential employer, assuming, of course, you have the desired background.

A résumé is intended to be brief. A CEO with decades of experience in business may have a multiple-page résumé, but a one-page executive summary highlighting his or her most pertinent accomplishments is likely to accompany it.

A CV, however, is supposed to lengthen over time. A CV generally includes the same general categories as seen on résumés, with the addition of often lengthy listings of publications and presentations. (This is, after all, a document targeted for academe, where "publish or perish" is the mantra for long-term survival.) As a result, CVs tend to be substantially longer than résumés.

In a CV, the academic background or education section is almost always presented first, a nod to its academic comfort zone, whereas in a well-written résumé related professional experience usually leads.

If you are applying for a position in an agency or a counseling center, you'll more than likely send a résumé. For research and faculty positions, the application process will usually require a CV. Outside of higher education and some research institutions, virtually all other professions use a résumé. We discuss a simple one- to two-page format for counselors seeking employment. There really are no magical formats. The best style is one that outlines your experience, accomplishments, and qualifications for the job.

BEWARE of "Cookie-Cutter" Résumés!

We provide several examples of résumés in this text, but we advise you to avoid taking these examples and simply plugging in your own information. You would probably not borrow your best friend's interview suit because it might not fit, and someone else's résumé could be just as ill fitting. Choose headings that make sense for *your* background. If your friend has written dozens of articles, then it makes sense that she would devote a section of her résumé or CV to publications. You might choose to highlight scholarships, volunteer work, or creative pursuits.

You may also choose to personalize your résumé by using a different typeface, by bolding and italicizing some sections, and by using bullet points. If you do, try to use a standard typeface—nothing quite so bold as **Broadway** or **Bauhaus 93**! Conventional typefaces include Times New Roman, Arial, **Franklin Gothic Medium**, and a number of other serif and sans serif types. Choose a streamlined typeface on the basis of its readability and recognize that the more unusual the typeface, the more likely you are to have trouble cutting and pasting it in an electronic application format.

How to Begin a Résumé

We suggest you develop a standard format, then edit according to the type of counseling position advertised. There are three general types of résumés:

1. *Chronological résumés* present work experience in a traditional, date-by-date format listing jobs, responsibilities, and accomplishments. Professionals using a chronological résumé usually have a significant amount of experience. Most job-seeking counselors, given their advanced education and degrees, will use this type of résumé.
2. *Functional résumés* present work experience by listing skills, education, and activities. Functional résumés are generally preferred by people with less job history (youth) or by people making a mid-career change (Bolles, 2004).
3. *Combination (or hybrid) format résumés* take elements of both chronological and functional résumés and *combine* them. This format is best used by job applicants who have had several similar jobs and wish to avoid redundancy in job descriptions and by those who are attempting a career change and want to highlight accomplishments related to the new career field without drawing attention to the jobs they've held. In both, skill-related accomplishments are usually followed by a list of previous positions or an employment history.

A Few Points Before You Begin Your Résumé or CV

1. *Your education and transferable skills are of critical importance.* Your experience, training, education, and skills serve as a bridge to desired employment. Make sure you design your résumé or CV in a manner that clearly highlights your training and skill areas.

2. *Claim the highest skills ethically possible.* For example, if you have co-facilitated counseling groups for 2 years, certainly list that. Do not, however, list that you developed and oversaw the group treatment model at your school or agency if this is untrue.

3. *Make your résumé or CV reader friendly.* Remember, when a search committee member first looks at your résumé or CV, he or she will give it a 30- to 45-second speed read (Bolles, 2007). If the search committee does a second viewing, they will spend considerably more time on it. Make sure your résumé or CV makes logical and chronological sense. Check for misspelled words, and have a career counselor or someone else you trust read it for content and mechanics.

4. *There is no one "right" résumé or CV format.* (There's a saying among career consultants—"Opinions about résumés are like bellybuttons. Everyone has a different one.") Make sure your résumé makes sense, flows logically, is factually accurate, and fits with the counseling position for which you have applied.

5. *Cover your most recent 8-10 years of work experience in the greatest detail, depending on your age and years in the field.* Faculty counselor education positions are different from positions in schools and agencies (especially in length). Do not be discouraged if you are a 25-year-old recent graduate of a counseling program. At your age and experience level, you are not expected to have long years of professional experience.

6. *Holding multiple jobs is no longer the problem it was in previous generations.* In this era, people are expected to hold three, four, or even more different jobs (Bolles, 2004). In higher education, the general understanding is that you must "move out to move up," and that is likely to be reflected in your CV.

7. *Be factually correct where your résumé or CV is concerned.* We emphasize this aspect of the job search throughout this text. You are responsible for anything you list in your résumé or CV. Promote your education, skills, training, and experience—just be sure to be honest. If you are caught lying on your résumé or CV, on a job application, or in an interview, the least you will lose is a job. In some cases, you may lose your career. Be advised!

Developing the Résumé

Identifying Information

All résumés should include your name, degree, license, certifications, address, and contact information (phone numbers and e-mail address).

Harriet Sanchez, MEd, NCC
445 Broadway Avenue
Washington, NY 14157
(817) 555-0123 (Cell)
E-Mail: Hsanchez@aol.com

or

Harriet Sanchez, MEd, NCC
445 Broadway Avenue, Washington, NY 14157
817.555.0123 | HSanchez@aol.com

A few words here about contact information:

- *Triple-check this information.* REALLY LOOK at it. Amy recently had a client who had to reprint her résumés because she didn't catch an error in her address.
- If you don't have an e-mail address, get one, and put it on your résumé. If you are engaged in a job search, check that e-mail account regularly (at least once a day). Most initial contact with candidates in today's job market is made via e-mail, and if you are not accessible through this communication tool, you may be counted out, even if you are extremely well qualified for a position.
- E-mail addresses should be professional-sounding. "Slinkybod@woohoo.com" is not likely to engender a lot of professional confidence. (Well, at least not in *this* profession.)
- What message will greet your caller on an unattended phone line? Does it sound professional? Is it possible a 3-year-old will pick up the phone? If your outbound message sounds like it was recorded during a frat party, it's time to change it, and if you share a phone with others who may not be trustworthy to take good messages, we have two words: *cell phone.*

Introduction

The next step involves selecting a job objective, which is simply the target position you are seeking. In the following example, Harriet is applying for a position as a school counselor.

Objective
Seeking a challenging position as a middle school counselor.

Or, she could simply address the advertised job:

Objective: Middle school counselor at Kennedy Middle School.

Both formats would be acceptable to most any search committee.

An alternative to a statement of objective is a professional summary, which is quickly gaining approval among career professionals. Here is another way Harriet might begin presenting her credentials:

Professional Summary

Nationally Certified Counselor (NCC #49346) with strengths in counseling at the middle-school level. Experience in developing student success programs and engaging parents in family conferences.

The professional summary can be used to specifically target elements of an employer's advertisement. Like an introductory paragraph, the professional summary serves as an introduction to what the reader will find if he or she reads the rest of the résumé. When written strategically, this statement can take great advantage of the 30 to 45 seconds the reviewer is likely to spend in his or her initial review.

Education

The next section for a counselor, given advanced education, would be to list education, degrees, licensure, and certifications.

Education

Oregon State University, Corvallis, OR, MEd, School Counseling, 2006–2008 (CACREP-accredited program)
Western Oregon University, Monmouth, OR, BA, Psychology, 2003–2006
Linn Benton Community College, Albany, OR, A.A., Psychology, 2001–2003

Another way to present this information would be to list degrees first:

Education

Master of Education in School Counseling (CACREP-accredited program), Oregon State University, Corvallis, Oregon (2008)
Bachelor of Arts in Psychology, Western Oregon University, Monmouth, Oregon (2006)
Associate of Arts, Linn Benton Community College, Albany, Oregon (2001–2003)

List all institutions attended, even if you did not earn a degree. Potential employers like to see a comprehensive list because it provides a tracking record of accomplishments. In some cases it's also possible the search committee may know someone at an institution where you studied, which could prove helpful for you.

Note: The education section of your résumé may be more effective in another location. Place this information near the top of your résumé if any of these conditions exist:

- You are applying for a position in an academic setting, especially in an institution of higher learning.
- You have recently completed an advanced degree that makes you eligible to compete for positions for which you would previously not have qualified.
- You have a degree, but not much work experience.

If none of these statements is applicable to your situation, it may be more effective for you to use this prime space to begin describing your accomplishments and other qualifications.

Licensure and Certification

Next list your license (if you have one) and national certification. If you are just graduating and lack both, then simply omit this section. Newly graduated or soon-to-graduate counselors are usually not expected to have their license or certification—at least not right away. Experienced counselors—those who have been out in the field for 3 or more years—will be expected to have either a license or certification, or both.

Certification
Nationally Certified Counselor (NCC #49346)

Employment History

The next section is the all-important section titled "Employment History." You might alternately name this section "Professional Experience," "Related Professional Experience," or "Counseling Experience," or use some other title that encapsulates what is contained within the text. This section will vary greatly given differences in age and life history. For younger counselors, or those just completing a graduate counseling degree, we suggest you list your practicum and internship as you would a job, but make it clear the experience was a practicum and internship. Also, highlight the skills and responsibilities you performed while on the job.

Employment History

Fall 2007–Spring 2008 Practicum–internship, Albany Middle School, Albany, OR.
- Responsible for providing individual and group counseling to students.
- Provided academic and personal counseling.
- Cofacilitated parent–counselor meetings.
- Assisted with school grief project.

2005–2008 Project Instructor, alternative school, Community Services Consortium, Albany, OR
- Provided individualized instruction to high school students.
- Used instruments such as the Test of Adult Basic Education as benchmarks.
- Provided tutoring in English, math, and reading skills.
- Provided career and academic counseling to students in school.

2003–2005 Resident Assistant in university residence hall, Western Oregon University, Monmouth, OR
- Responsible for oversight of 20 students on floor.
- Provided health and safety programming information.
- Served as liaison and referral resource for the counseling center, health services, and career center.

- Served on diverse team of resident advisors representing four countries.
- Developed Third Ear, a peer helping resource supervised by the counseling center.

An alternate way to present the same information would be

Counseling Practicum (Academic year 2007–2008), Albany Middle School, Albany, OR

- Provided individual and group counseling to students for academic and personal issues.
- Cofacilitated parent–counselor meetings.
- Assisted in development of school grief project in response to the unexpected death of a student.

Project Instructor, Alternative School, **Community Services Consortium**, Albany, OR (2005–2008)

- Provided individualized instruction to high school students.
- Used benchmarking tools, including Test of Adult Basic Education.
- Counseled students in regard to academics and vocational choice.

Resident Assistant, Western Oregon University, Monmouth, OR (2003–2005)

- Represented Residence Education Department to 20 residents of university housing, providing health and safety programming, referral to student services, and on-site emergency assistance.
- Served as liaison and referral source for counseling center, health services, and career center.
- Developed Third Ear, a peer helping resource supervised by the Counseling Center.

Summary of Qualifications

It may be advisable to include a summary of qualifications on your résumé if you desire to highlight special skills, training, additional coursework, or any other additional information that could strengthen your qualifications for the job.

Summary of Qualifications
- More than 5 years counseling, tutoring, and assessing students in educational settings.
- Excellent references at the alternative school and on the practicum–internship
- Trained in solution-focused school counseling during practicum–internship

- Served on multidisciplinary committees, assisting with Individualized Education Programs, staffing for special education students, and working with discipline issues
- Extensive experience in using computer-based systems for counseling, advising, testing, and presenting psychoeducational workshops (PowerPoint)

Honors, Awards, Professional Memberships, and So Forth

Next, we suggest you list any honors you may have won or honorary organizations into which you were inducted.

Different candidates will handle this information in different ways. Because you don't want a cookie-cutter résumé, review the information you want to present and identify titles that most effectively present it.

A "rule of three" may be helpful to you in determining how many different sections you need to present here. For example, if you have earned a number of scholarships or academic awards, you may want to have a section called "Special Academic Achievements." Any time you have three or more similar awards that can be grouped together, do so. If the list is long and you can shorten it by regrouping—again, in groups of three or more—that may prove effective as well.

Don't create a section called "Academic Awards" if you only have one award to list. In this case, you might want to include it in your education section.

Be sure to list professional memberships. Membership in the American Counseling Association (ACA) and the relevant professional counseling division demonstrates that you are interested in long-term professional development, reading journal articles, staying abreast of developments in your profession, and supporting your national professional organizations.

An honors section may look something like this:

Honors
> Member of Chi Sigma Iota (National Counseling honorary), 2008–present
> Member of Psi Chi (National Psychology honorary), 2006–present

Professional Memberships
> American Counseling Association, 2006–present
> American School Counselors Association, 2006–present

Hobbies and Interests

Listing hobbies and interests is a good way to add some personal interest to your résumé, especially if you have some unused space. Employers might desire to know more about you, and hobbies provide a window into you as a person. Hobbies are also how people renew their energy levels, provide emotional stability, and keep themselves healthy and balanced.

You never know when a hobby could be the tipping point for getting a job offer, either. Once I (Shannon) was offered a job partially on the basis of having been a competitive softball player. It seems the agency was putting together a co-rec team and thought a good left fielder was an asset. Naturally, my background on the softball diamond was not the main reason I got the job, but it did help crack open the employment door just a little.

Amy weighing in here, as well: Don't list hobbies in which you really have no interest. Once, as I was reviewing a student's résumé, I asked about her interest in golf. She told me, "Oh, I don't really play golf. Somebody just told me that would be a good thing to put on my résumé." Realize that if it's on your résumé, you can expect a question about it, so make sure your enthusiasm for your hobbies is real!

Hobbies and Interests
Running, traveling, and competitive softball

References

You've probably seen the following on many résumés:

References
Available on request

It's not really necessary.

Nevertheless, you'll see this on many résumés, and if you have space at the bottom of yours, you'll probably add it on, as well. But if you don't have room for it, don't stress.

Employers assume that if you are qualified and interviewed, you will be able to provide three to five names of people who will enthusiastically endorse your candidacy for the position for which you have applied. "References available on request" is akin to "The End." When you reach this part of the résumé, it's as though you are saying, "That's it. All of the most relevant information I could think of to present to you regarding my candidacy for your open position has preceded these four words."

When you are asked for references, use the same header that you've used on your résumé and cover letter, which, of course, includes your name and all relevant contact information, then list *on a separate page* those professionals who have agreed to serve as references on your behalf, listing their names, titles, institutions or organizations, and all of *their* relevant contact information.

A sample résumé demonstrating appropriate format and presentation appears on pages 41–42.

The Model CV

The principle difference between a résumé and a CV is length. *Vita* literally means "life" in Latin, and a CV is a summary of your life.

The concept of "one correct CV format" is an ongoing myth. CVs vary depending on the field, individual experience, type of academic position being sought, and numerous other variables. We suggest a CV format that is simple and offer recommendations of what should and should not go into a CV. Remember, many of today's senior faculty entered a very different type of academic job market in their era. In fact, because of the powerful influence of the Internet, academia is rapidly evolving (distance education, overseas education, multiple campuses, Web-based instruction, etc.). As you create your CV, you

Harriet Sanchez, MEd, NCC

445 Broadway Avenue • Washington, NY 14157
(817) 555-0123 (c) • Hsanchez@aol.com

Profile

Master's-educated Nationally Certified Counselor (NCC #49346) seeking school counseling position at middle school level.

Summary of Qualifications

- More than 5 years experience counseling, tutoring, and assisting students in educational settings
- Trained and experienced in solution-focused school counseling during practicum–internship
- Served on multidisciplinary committees assisting with Individualized Education Programs, staffed special education cases, and worked with disciplinary issues
- Extensive experience in using computer-based systems for counseling, advising, testing, and presenting psychoeducational workshops

Professional Education

Master of Education in School Counseling (2008)
Oregon State University, Corvallis, OR (CACREP-accredited program)
Bachelor of Arts in Psychology (2006)
Western Oregon University, Monmouth, OR
Additional college credit earned in Psychology (2001–2002)
Linn-Benton Community College, Albany, OR

Related Experience

School Counseling Practicum–Internship (2007–2008)
Albany Middle School, Albany, OR
- Provided individual and group counseling to students, including academic and personal counseling
- Cofacilitated parent–counselor meetings
- Assisted with school grief project

Project Instructor (2005–present)
Alternative school, Community Services Consortium, Albany, OR
- Provided individualized instruction to at-risk high school students
- Used Test of Adult Basic Education and other assessment tools as benchmarks for student progress.
- Tutored students in English, math, and reading skills
- Counseled students in alternative school in career and academic decision-making process

Resident Assistant (2003–2005)
University Residence Hall, Western Oregon University, Monmouth, OR
- Developed Third Ear, a peer helping organization supervised by the counseling center

(Continued)

Harriet Sanchez, MEd, NCC

Page 2

Resident Assistant (Continued)

- Supported and managed life skills activities for 20 students on floor
- Coordinated health and safety programming
- Served as liaison and referral resource to counseling center, career center, and health services
- Selected for diverse team of resident advisors representing four countries in developing cultural diversity programming

Honors

Member of Chi Sigma Iota (National Counseling honorary), 2008–present
Member of Psi Chi (National Psychology honorary), 2008–present

Professional Memberships

American Counseling Association
American School Counselors Association

Hobbies and Interests

Running, traveling, and competitive softball

References

Available on request

---

need to understand that it is a living document that will need to adapt and change to keep pace with this dynamic era. We offer a sample CV and encourage you to tailor yours accordingly as your own career moves forward.

Length

As previously suggested, there are few hard-and-fast rules to CV construction. The length of a CV is mostly related to years in the field and number of publications and presentations. Pages can add up quickly after only a few years in a teaching or academic research position, so don't be dismayed when comparing your thin CV with your advisor's hefty, *War and Peace*–sized document. (*Note:* If your CV can no longer be stapled with even an industrial-strength stapler, you may consider editing a bit.) Your initial competition is with your peers, seldom with experienced professionals.

CV Format and Content

Despite variations, all CVs have three basic elements in common:

- Name, address, and contact information
- Education, degrees, and certifications
- Professional and related experience

Your name, address, telephone number (cell and landline, if you have one), and e-mail address should be listed at the top of the CV. For consistency and to avoid confusion, the name you use on your CV should be consistent with that on official documents, otherwise discrepancies could arise and cast suspicion on you. If you answer to your middle name or a nickname, put that name in quotation marks. If you have changed your surname, but your previous surname is retained on transcripts, publications, and such, be sure to notify the search committee of this change.

(Shannon's the expert on CVs, but I'm going to jump in here because he's never *personally* experienced this, and I have. In the case of professionals who have married or legally changed their name and are now known professionally by their married name, it is advisable to include the original surname on the CV. In my case, I earned my degrees while I was still Amy K. Reece, but I have adopted "Amy Reece Connelly"—without a hyphen—as my professional name, even though most people know me as "Amy Connelly." The high rate of divorce and remarriage is probably partially responsible for the number of women choosing to retain their original names, at least professionally, to avoid long-term confusion.)

Education and Degrees

Your CV should include a record of all undergraduate and graduate education and degrees, including

- academic area of specialization;
- names and locations of institutions you attended; and
- dates the degree or certification was conferred.

It is still an advantage to list attendance at institutions at which no degree was earned because you may have received specialized training or formed relationships with faculty who might be helpful to your search.

Professional and Related Experience

Your experience will become the most important section of your CV and, more important, your professional life. Under this section, list everything that relates to the career you are seeking. For example, if you are seeking an assistant professor position in school counseling, list not only professional experience in school counseling but also anything related. Perhaps you were a behavioral management specialist at a public or private school in addition to serving as a school counselor.

This section of the CV is one place where you should engage in name-dropping. Our experience has been that many counselor educators are reluctant to resort to such "shameless" self-promotion. Our contention is that it's fair to list anything that makes your CV stronger, *provided the information is accurate*. The past few years have witnessed a number of high-profile cases of well-known people caught embellishing their résumé or CV. Our advice is this: Be ready to verify and defend anything you put in your CV. If you cannot do this, the least it will cost you is a job. At most, misrepresentation could lead to legal charges and ruin your career.

Regarding degrees, never list yourself as having a degree until you have met all degree requirements and been awarded the degree. If you have passed all requirements but the degree has not yet been conferred, include a brief explanation that all requirements have been met and the date on which the degree will be conferred.

> *Proper format:*
>> Doctoral Student, Postmodern State University. Dissertation successfully defended April 30, 2008. Degree to be conferred May 15, 2008.
>
> *Improper format:*
>> PhD Student at Creative Embellishment Institution. Anticipated completion May 2009.

CV Categories

Categories are subheadings in the CV that lend more explanation to your experience, training, and education. Choose CV categories that emphasize your strengths and achievements. This list includes a variety of category examples you might use for your CV:

Education	Academic Background
Professional Studies	Areas of Expertise
Certification	Graduate Teaching/Research Assistantships
Degrees	Teaching Experience
Dissertation	Counseling Experience
Major Area	Overseas Experience
Minor Area	Career Highlights
Master's Thesis	Consulting
Service	Awards
Publications	Books
Journal Articles	Professional Memberships
Editorial Boards	Conference Presentations
Committee Chair	Major Committees
Foreign Languages	Computer Skills

The possibilities are almost limitless. The critical issue is how you market these areas in your CV. Use active rather than passive voice.

Action Words

The headings and words you use to describe your experience, counseling philosophy, and qualifications are your voice to the reader. Concise, direct, descriptive communication is your goal. The CV is not the place for elongated, eloquent phrases. Be thorough but brief. Remember, in the initial screening of a résumé or CV, the reader spends less than a minute (Bolles, 2004). In fact, given the length of the initial screening of a CV, brevity may to some degree be advantageous.

Unlike an article for, say, the *Journal of Counseling & Development*, sentence fragments are acceptable, even preferable in CVs. Fragments allow expressive freedom and brevity. For example, "Coordinated an ACA Presentation on PTSD" concisely and effectively conveys the same information as "I was responsible for the organization of a national presentation on PTSD." Action words help craft a more interesting, lively, and dynamic CV. Here are some sample action words to assist you in preparing your CV:

Accomplished	Facilitated
Achieved	Founded
Advised	Implemented
Assessed	Initiated
Assisted	Integrated
Authored	Lectured
Awarded	Monitored
Chaired	Negotiated
Coauthored	Organized
Collaborated	Planned
Completed	Presented
Consulted	Presided
Coordinated	Published
Counseled	Reorganized
Designed	Researched
Developed	Revised
Directed	Screened
Diagnosed	Standardized
Drafted	Supervised
Edited	Taught
Established	Updated
Evaluated	Verified

Note that the phrase "responsible for" is not on this list. "Responsible for," although used frequently, possibly even overused, is passive and not recommended. You could be "responsible for" something, but never quite get around to doing it. Choose an action word instead!

Drafting the CV

When making the initial draft of your CV, don't concern yourself with length, style, and so forth. Get the basic information on paper in sections, then go back and edit. In fact, the editing is what makes the CV appealing.

Creating CV Categories

Heading

Any writer will tell you that the best place to begin a story is at the beginning. In creating the CV, that means including your name, degrees, licenses, certifications, address, phone number (cell and landline), and e-mail address at the very top of your CV.

Janice Rogers, Doctoral Candidate, MS, LMHC, NCC
439 Winwood Dr.
El Paso, TX 79997
(915) 555-2101
E-mail: jrrogers@verizon.net

Mission Statement

Some academics will list a mission statement under that heading. Academics do this to explain their philosophical approach as a counselor educator or clinical supervisor. Personal mission statements are optional. If you use one, make it brief, and be sure it accurately reflects your approach. You do not want your references contradicting you in this vein.

> *Academic Mission Statement:* Offering a constructivist, social justice teaching and counseling philosophy to a global, multicultural cohort of graduate students

Education and Degrees

Your education should come next because search committees will want to know the institution at which you did your graduate work. Higher education is very communal in that people either know faculty at a given counselor education program or they know of said faculty and the nature of the program. Your institution's counselor education program establishes some baseline of information about you. Putting education and degrees in a prominent place on page 1 also establishes that you have the necessary qualifications for the job.

> *Doctoral Candidate,* Counselor Education, University of Texas El Paso, El Paso, TX. *Dissertation Topic:* Divorce and recovery among graduate students in counselor education programs. Expected graduation May 2009.
>
> *MS,* Marriage and Family Counseling, Northern Arizona University, Flagstaff, AZ. Conferred June 2005.
>
> *BA,* Psychology, Southern Oregon State College, Ashland, OR. Conferred June 2003.

Some applicants dress this section up by including major and minor professor and the like. This may be interpreted as extraneous, and furthermore, your major professor should be one of your references, thus making her or his mention in this section unnecessary.

Licensure, Certifications, or Advanced Training

This section provides you, the applicant, with an opportunity to list important credentials you have or will soon earn. Counselor education programs are always pleased to have applicants holding licensure, national certification, and so forth. Advanced training can add to your CV, emphasizing ongoing credentialing.

LMFC, Licensed Marriage and Family Counselor (Arizona)
NCC, Nationally Certified Counselor
NBCC, National Board for Certified Counselors
Certified Divorce Mediator, Arizona State Certified
Solution Focused Brief Therapy Intensive, El Paso, TX, October 2006

Caution: If you put down that you have a license or certification, you must have completed all requirements and have it in hand. If you are working on licensure, simply write, "Have completed supervised clock hour requirements and will sit for the exam November 18," or whatever is the case.

Research Interests

This heading provides the opportunity to signal your particular areas of research interest. For beginning faculty who may have published little or none at all, it establishes future intentions. Naturally, your dissertation title will signal where your current interests lie. Some newly minted PhDs and doctoral students may have copublished articles with faculty, thus creating a stronger track record. Whatever the case, list your research interests:

> Counseling female high school students with self-injurious
> behaviors, ethical issues in school counseling, and efficacy
> of peer helping programs.

Professional Experience

This is the most critical section of the CV (well, of equal importance to the publication section) because it provides search committees the basis for whether to keep your CV in the job search or to screen you out. Because the committee doesn't know you (except in rare instances), experience (and a well-crafted CV) is what keeps your candidacy moving forward. List your professional counseling and counselor education experience, beginning with your most current position. If your current position is that of a doctoral student in counseling education, list that and what duties you have performed.

Professional Experience
Doctoral Student, University of Northern Colorado, Greeley, CO,
Fall 2004–current
- Graduate Teaching Assistant teaching Counseling Skills lab
  (two per year) to master's-level students in school and
  community counseling
- Dissertation topic: Treatment of self-injurious behaviors in
  high schools
- Cotaught career counseling with Professor Don Henley (2 years)
- Doctoral student on master's-degree student's portfolio defense
- Doctoral internship in university counseling center, 2005–2006
  Individual and group counseling and personal,
  career, and academic counseling. Ran support groups for
  students recovering from sexual abuse

- Doctoral internship in Career Center (2005–2006)
- Delivered guest lectures in counseling theory, family counseling, and assessment in counseling
- Published a peer-review article, "Self-Injurious Behaviors in Adolescents," in the *Journal of Mental Heath Counseling* (see publications section)
- Coauthored "Ethical Considerations for Middle School Counselors" with Professor Laticia Franz in *Professional School Counseling*

School Counselor, Midvale High School, Midvale, AZ, 2000–2004

- Responsible for individual and group counseling of students
- Extensive personal, career, and academic counseling experience
- Cochaired multidisciplinary team of school counselors, school social workers, school psychologist, and special education teachers
- Implemented, trained, and supervised student peer helping volunteers
- Vice president, local school counselor's organization

The preceding represents a basic approach to the professional experience section.

Publications

The publications section of the CV is equally as important as the experience section. This represents a departure from CVs for counselors working in schools and clinics because counseling experience would be the primary issue of interest for K–12 schools and mental health clinics. Because tenure and reputations are made through research and publications, scholarly activity, or the potential for such, will weigh heavily on the minds of most search committees, particularly those in counselor education programs with doctoral programs. Aspiring counselor educators holding doctoral degrees from lesser known institutions or nontraditional institutions (e.g., Web-based universities) need not feel the job market is closed to them. For counselor educators, indeed for all faculty, publishing is the great equalizer in higher education. Counselor educators want to demonstrate to search committees that they have the potential for scholarly activity. The best way to demonstrate scholarly activity is to have a history of scholarly activity. In lieu of publications, counselor educators in the job market need to be able to list and discuss various research interests. Now, this advice may come as elementary (as the famed sleuth Sherlock Holmes would opine in prosaic fashion), but as an experienced counselor educator and veteran of academic search committees, I (Shannon) can tell you that not every counselor education candidate knows this.

The higher education landscape has also changed drastically in the past decade because newly minted PhDs and EdDs are expected to have at least one scholarly publication when going into the job market. In previous eras, publications would have been the exception for doctoral students. In the event you are a new or soon-to-be PhD or EdD counselor educator, our advice is to get going on a viable publication in a peer-reviewed journal or author or coauthor a book chapter. National newsletters are okay venues, but a huge factor in search committees' decision making will be the candidate's ability to publish and earn tenure. It's much easier to establish yourself as a viable scholar when you have scholarly publications. Academic history is chock full of potential scholars who for whatever reason could not seem to meet scholarly demands. Fortunately, many doctoral counselor education programs require their students to submit at least one manuscript to a scholarly journal. Naturally, in some counselor education programs, the major professor will take a doctoral student under her or his wing and copublish a scholarly article. However, such examples of teaching doctoral students the craft of publishing are not as universal as many believe. If you are contemplating applying for doctoral study in counselor education, we suggest you inquire about publication requirements or opportunities during your doctoral study.

Professional Presentations

Presentations at national conferences such as that of the American Counseling Association (ACA) represent an opportunity for gaining professional development, networking, and building your strength as a professional. Although national presentations count less than scholarly publications, they do help bolster your case as an active professional. Presenting also provides you an opportunity to network with faculty. For doctoral students, presenting at state and regional conventions represents a good beginning, although working up to national presentations at meetings of the ACA, American School Counselor Association (ASCA), American Mental Health Counselors Association (AMHCA), and so forth should be your goal. Again, doctoral programs in counselor education have a responsibility to prepare future counselor educators to present at venues such as national conferences.

Professional Memberships

When preparing for a counselor education job search, memberships in professional associations are an absolute must. Most readers already know this, but in the event you don't, here are our suggestions. At a minimum, you need to join ACA and the Association of Counselor Education and Supervision (ACES), and you should join the ACA affiliate representing your particular counseling specialty (e.g., ASCA, AMHCA, or American Rehabilitation Counselors Association [ARCA]). If you have been a member of Chi Sigma Iota, the national counseling honorary, be certain to list that because many counselor education programs have such chapters. List these and all other memberships (such as state and local counseling organizations) in this section. If you do not have memberships in these areas, make sure you get them ASAP. Do not list a membership in an organization unless you are current member in good standing.

Honors and Awards

Have you won awards related to the counseling profession or as a graduate student? Were you selected as your program's doctoral student of the year? Did you win a prestigious graduate student award at your university? If you were a counselor in a school or agency and won an award, list that as well. Again, list only awards that you actually won. This would seem elementary, but Shannon knows of one person who, lacking any awards, actually created a fictitious one and listed himself as the winner. Discovery of such dishonesty can end a career before it begins.

References

Most counselor education programs will want letters of recommendation, but list your references on an addendum page as well. There is some question as to how many references should be included, and a general guideline is no less than three and no more than five. Three references is the usual standard, although we have noticed academic ads in the *Chronicle of Higher Education* and *Counseling Today* that require five references. *Always ask* before listing someone as a reference. You would be surprised to know how many people simply list references but have never bothered to solicit that reference's approval. Should a search committee member call and discover you never received approval from a reference, your candidacy is sunk! You also don't want a lukewarm letter of reference because such amounts to being damned with faint praise. So, get references from faculty who will give you a robust recommendation.

On the following page is an example of an appropriately formatted CV that can be used as a model.

Again, your CV does not need to be packed with minutiae; in fact, a veteran of many academic search committees can easily see when applicants are "padding their stats" with minor and sometimes irrelevant information. List the information that relates to the career at hand (counselor education), which means degrees, committees, publications, and so forth. The most critical information for your candidacy is the doctoral degree (or a date for dissertation defense), publications, and classes you have taught or cotaught or for which you have served as the graduate teaching assistant.

Writing the Cover Letter

The term *cover letter* is somewhat vague and in reality a misnomer. The cover letter serves to highlight the knowledge, skills, and dispositions outlined in your CV or résumé. When a search committee receives your CV or résumé and cover letter, the screener skims your résumé or CV and then proceeds to do the same with your cover letter. The function of a cover letter is to present your résumé or CV but also to make a personal statement to the search committee of why you are a good fit for their agency, school, or counselor education department . Your résumé or CV serves to

- introduce you;
- outline your qualifications; and
- stimulate interest in your qualifications, background, and training.

Angela M. Rogers, PhD, LMHC, NCC

429 Wentworth Avenue
State College, PA 14009
(716) 287-8423 (h) • (716) 543-9021 (c)
amrogers@email.org

Academic Mission Statement: Striving to offer a constructivist, social justice approach to counselor education to prepare future counselors for a pluralistic, meta-cultural world.

Education and Degrees

PhD, Counselor Education, Pennsylvania State University, State College, PA. Conferred May 2009 (CACREP-accredited program)
Dissertation Topic: Efficacy of court-mandated conjoint martial therapy
Minor: Marriage and Family Counseling

MS, Marriage and Family Counseling, University of Connecticut, Storrs, CT. June 2001

BA, Psychology, University of Minnesota—Morris, Morris, MN. May 1999. Graduated Summa Cum Laude and was selected by UMM faculty as a Scholar of the College.
Minor: Anthropology

Licensure/Certification/Advanced Trainings

LMHC, Licensed Mental Health Counselor (Connecticut, New York)
NCC, Nationally Certified Counselor, National Board for Certified Counselors (NBCC)
Solution Focused Therapy Intensive, Chicago, IL. June 2006
Certified Mediator, Commonwealth of Pennsylvania

Research Interests

Marriage and relationship therapy, cultural competence in play therapy, Internet counseling with couples

Professional Experience

Doctoral program, Pennsylvania State University, State College, PA (Fall 2005–Spring 2009)
- Taught Counseling Skills lab for master's-degree students (2 years)
- GTA for Career Counseling (3 years)
- GTA in University Counseling Center, Pennsylvania State University (2006–2007)
- Assisted Prof. Mary Shriner with national research study on depression
- Graded papers and delivered guest lecturers for several graduate counseling classes
- Served as graduate representative to Counselor Education faculty

(Continued)

Angela M. Rogers, PhD, LMHC, NCC (Page 2)

Professional Experience (Continued)

Marriage and Family Counselor, Looking Glass Counseling Center, Danbury, CT (2001–2005)
- Counseled couples and families in large outpatient mental health clinic
- Ran Parent Effectiveness Trainings for teen parents
- Wrote reports to Social Services and area courts
- Supervisor for Continuing Education

Opportunities Unlimited, Inc., Morris, MN (1997–1999)
- Case manager in human services agency serving developmentally disabled population
- Managed caseload of 25
- Provided occupational skills training for clients in supportive work placements
- Advocated for rights of developmentally disabled clients

Teaching Assistant, Psychology discipline, University of Minnesota—Morris, Morris, MN (1998–1999)
- Cofacilitated lab sections of Ethics for the Human Services and Abnormal Psychology
- Attended and cofacilitated weekly TA discussion meetings
- Copresented "The Undergraduate Teaching Assistant's Experience" at the Minnesota Psychology Association's annual conference, St. Paul, MN

Publications

Franz, L., & Rogers, A. (2007). Ethical considerations for middle school counselors. *Professional School Counseling, 21*, 50–66.

Rogers, A. (2006). Self-injurious behavior in adolescents. *Journal of Mental Health Counseling, 30*, 55–67.

Rogers, A. (2004). Book review of D. Becvar's *In the presence of Grief: Helping family members resolve death, dying, and bereavement issues. Family Journal, 26*, 77–80.

Professional Presentations

2007, March, Art therapy in family counseling. Presented at the American Counseling Association meeting, Detroit, MI. Copresenter with Rigoberto Muniz.

2006, April, Helping children cope with the death of a parent. Presented at the Pennsylvania State Conference on Grief Counseling, Pittsburgh, PA.

2005, October, Play therapy in elementary schools: Supporting the academic and developmental mission. In-service for State College school district. Copresenter with April Anderson and Jim Jones.

2005, July, Art therapy with adults: A creative approach. Presented at the American Mental Health Counselors Association national conference, Washington, DC.

(Continued)

Angela M. Rogers, PhD, LMHC, NCC (Page 3)

Editorial Review Boards
Journal of the Pennsylvania Counseling Association. Term: 2006–2008

Professional Memberships
American Counseling Association
American Mental Health Counselors Association
Association for Counselor Education and Supervision
Pennsylvania Counseling Association

Honors and Awards
Counselor Education Graduate Student of the Year, University of
Connecticut, Storrs, CT, 2001
Scholar of the College, University of Minnesota—Morris, 1999
Chancellor's Scholarship, University of Minnesota—Morris, 1996

References
Ernest Borgnine, PhD, Associate Professor, Counselor Education,
Pennsylvania State University, State College, PA 16802,
(814) 867-0400, e-mail: eborg@psu.edu
Jane Objii, EdD, Associate Professor, Counselor Education,
Pennsylvania State University, State College, PA 16802,
(814) 867-0401, e-mail: jobjii@psu.edu
Gillian Karol, PhD, Professor, Department Chair, Counselor Education,
Pennsylvania State University, State College, PA 16802,
(804) 867-0402, e-mail: gcarol@psu.edu

Creativity is an asset in writing a cover letter, but don't overly concern yourself with catchy phrases or an attention-getting style. Imagine you are speaking directly to the reader. Your tone should be professional but conversational in nature. In addition, hit the highlights and resist the temptation to cram everything you have in your résumé or CV.

Regarding length, the cover letter should definitely be limited to two pages. We have seen cover letters that go on for four-plus pages and believe us, wily and battered veterans of far too many search committees, such self-aggrandizing about one's qualifications does not help a candidacy! It's also likely a reader will stop after two pages. (*Amy's note:* When presenting a résumé for positions not in academe, a cover letter should not exceed *one* page!)

In the early stages of a job search, you may send a cover letter to inquire about future openings. This is acceptable in higher education, in schools, in college counseling, and for counselor education positions. This strategy also presents you with the opportunity for contact with future potential colleagues who will be in a hiring mode at some point in the future. In fact, according to Bolles (2007), today's professional will change jobs more often than those of previous generations.

When a counseling position has been advertised, a letter of application, along with a copy of your résumé or CV, is your entry into the pool of applications. Use your letter to match your skills and interests with those of the advertised position description. Describe your achievements confidently, but refrain from overinflation, stilted prose, or long sentences unless this is truly representative of your writing style. The cover letter is your means of expressing your interest in the position, highlighting your qualifications, and promoting your candidacy.

The cover letter is also a screening device. Along with the CV, it may be circulated to each member of the search committee. Some committees will read every document submitted by each applicant. In other committees, someone will screen out less qualified applicants, leaving the committee to screen only the most qualified. It's impossible to predict the exact role your cover letter will play in the application process, although our experience is that it is usually important. A thoughtful, insightful application letter can certainly be an asset to an application. Conversely, a wordy, dry letter can sink your candidacy.

It should go without saying that your application letter must be grammatically correct. If you have earned an advanced degree, your communication skills in your native language are expected to be superior to those of the general population. Both of us have seen candidates dismissed from further consideration because of poorly written letters of application. In this era of electronic communication, you are well advised to pay attention to the quality of writing in e-mails, as well. Review carefully before hitting the send button!

We recommend you write a first draft, then reread it and edit appropriately. Before you send it out, have someone you know to be a good editor read it to catch errors and to ensure that it makes sense.

Addressing the Cover Letter

Send your letter to the person identified as the search committee chair or personnel representative. If no name is listed or if the advertisement directs you to address the department, address your letter to the committee at large or the personnel committee. (If you're up to some sleuthing, you could also contact the departmental administrator and request the name of the person who is chairing the committee.) Some career search experts may advise you to avoid salutations altogether for jobs for which no specific person is listed. From our perspective as career counselors and as professionals with almost 4 decades' combined experience serving on search committees, letters without a salutation seem incomplete. When you choose a salutation, however, use one that accurately reflects the current era.

Possible Salutations
- Dear Chair (gender neutral)
- Dear Chairman
- Dear Chairwoman
- Dear Search Committee Chair
- Dear Search Committee (plural when unspecified)
- Dear Personnel Officer (unspecified)
- To the Search Committee

Salutations to Avoid

- Dear Gentlemen (sexist)
- Dear Madam (archaic)
- Dear Reader (too generic)
- Dear Friend (too informal)
- To Whom It May Concern (too impersonal)
- Dear Lady (well . . . perhaps this was useful during the Victorian era!)

Some Tips on Cover Letter Etiquette

- Use a laser printer for crispness and clarity of print.
- Choose stationery that matches your résumé or CV.
- Use 12-point type. (Anything smaller than this may force aging professors in denial about their diminishing eyesight to reach for reading glasses.)
- Whenever possible, address the cover letter to a specific person, and be sure you have correctly identified that person's title.
- Use a salutation like those in the preceding list if no person is specified in the ad.
- Begin your letter with a statement of intent as a formal candidate, and state the position title.
- As a courtesy, state how you learned of the vacancy (e.g., newspaper, electronic mailing list, *Counseling Today*, etc.)
- Refer to pertinent information about the school, college, agency, and so forth.
- Emphasize your experience and whatever skills you have that relate to the position.
- Be thorough, though concise. The cover letter should be no more than two pages long.
- Proofread and edit c-a-r-e-f-u-l-l-y! Grammatical errors will sink your candidacy.
- Keep a copy of the letter and CV or résumé for your records.

Sample letters of application appear on the following pages.

Sample Letter of Application

March 12, 2009
1339 Highland Drive
Morningside, AR 72577

Personnel Department
Bethesda School District
2555 Ravenwood Way
Hickory, AR 72577

Dear Personnel Officer:

Please consider me as an applicant for the school counseling position at Bethesda High School. I noticed the advertisement in the February 17 edition of the *Arkansas Democrat-Gazette*. Currently, I am a graduate student completing my studies at Arkansas State University and will graduate this May with a master's degree in school counseling. In addition to general course work, I have completed 700 hours of field experience in a public high school and also have 4 years experience teaching in an alternative school.

During my studies at Arkansas State University, I was selected as the graduate student of the year for 2008–2009, was president of Chi Sigma Iota (the counseling honorary), and presented at the Arkansas State counseling conference in Little Rock last October. This past academic year, I also served an internship at the Arkansas State University Career Center, assisting undergraduate and graduate students in writing résumés and cover letters and practicing interviewing.

My practicum and internship was at Truman High School, where I assisted the counseling staff with academic, career, and personal counseling. There, I cofacilitated two groups for students at risk of dropping out, running an after-school support group for single parents and assisting with career counseling in the Teen Parent Program sponsored by Truman High School.

My résumé and the three letters of reference requested in the advertisement are being forwarded from the Career Center at Arkansas State University. I would welcome the opportunity to discuss this position with you in person. Should you have additional questions for me, please feel free to contact me any time at (870) 471-1777 or via e-mail at jrogers@aol.com.

Respectfully,

John Rogers

John Rogers

Sample Letter of Application

March 28, 2009
427 Collingwood Drive
Lincoln, NY 14164

Mary Sanchez, MS, LMHC
Manager
Child & Family Services
1444 Heartbreak Boulevard
Pencil Point, NJ 14444

Dear Ms. Sanchez:

Please consider me as an applicant for the mental health counselor position at Child & Family Services. I noticed the advertisement in *The Buffalo News*. For the past 4 years, I have been an addictions counselor with the Sunlight Recovery Clinic in Buffalo, NY, counseling individuals, groups, and families. I will also complete my master's in mental health counseling at Niagara University in May of this year.

In addition to my counseling experience at Sunlight, I have completed a 1,000-hour field experience at Child & Adolescent Treatment Services (CATS) in Buffalo, NY, where I counseled children and adolescents using both individual and group counseling. During my field experience, I cofacilitated sexual abuse recovery groups for adolescents and helped design a 16-week treatment program for adolescents with eating disorders. At CATS, I was trained and supervised in dialectical behavioral therapy (DBT) and also presented the DBT model at the New York Counseling Association annual conference in Saratoga Springs, NY.

My complete file, including three letters of recommendation, is being forwarded to you from the Career Center at Niagara University. Should you have additional questions, feel free to contact me any time at (716) 745-7798 or via e-mail at triciawashington@aol.com.

Respectfully,

Tricia Washington

Tricia Washington

Chapter

Preparing and Planning for an Interview

Congratulations! You Have an Interview!

Finally! All of the meticulous work you've put into developing a strong résumé and crafting an informative cover letter (not to mention the education and experience you've garnered) are beginning to pay off. You have an interview for your dream job. You can already envision yourself on your first day on the job behind your own desk with your own phone, your own computer, and your nameplate on the door!

Whoa, there, Nelly! Before you get carried away, you still have a lot of preparation to do for your interview before you can start cashing a paycheck. In fact, preparing for the interview is probably *the* most crucial stage of the job search and one many aspiring job seekers do not put enough work into (Bolles, 2007).

We tell our students and clients that just as actors rehearse for stage productions and athletes drill in preparation for games, job seekers should practice for interviews. Legendary University of California, Los Angeles, basketball coach John Wooden (2005) had a saying: "Failing to prepare is preparing to fail" (p. 158). Following this sage advice, we outline a sample strategy for you to follow:

- Prepare
- Execute
- Follow up
- Receive offer
- Evaluate
- Negotiate
- Accept or reject offer

Your First Contact With the Organization

More often than not, your first encounter with an organization that shows interest in your application will be by e-mail or telephone. The more important consideration for you as a job seeker is that the organization's first impression of you could be formed by how their initial contact is received and your response to it.

Listen to your outgoing phone message on any telephone line that you have provided to potential employers. Do you sound energized and upbeat? Are there distracting noises in the background? Is the outgoing message appropriate and professional? Is your message up to date?

How often do you check your e-mail? If you're in the middle of a job search, you should be checking at least once a day, and probably more often than that. Are you responsive to the organization's needs? If they are trying to schedule a phone interview during the next week, if you are truly interested you will find some time within those parameters to make it work. They may not be able to wait for 2 weeks until after you've returned from your third cousin's wedding in Sheboygan . . . or your own wedding, for that matter.

Here is a real-life, recent hiring experience that illustrates the importance of this initial contact:

> Our organization was intent on finding a career counselor for a specific geographic area who could support individuals relocating to the area, primarily through phone and e-mail contact.
>
> Several of the candidates who applied seemed very promising but were eliminated from consideration for a variety of reasons. One candidate submitted a bio that had no contact information other than his name. We contacted no fewer than three candidates through their e-mail addresses requesting time for a phone interview, without response. One candidate for this position didn't have an e-mail address listed on her résumé, and the outgoing message on her home phone line was so lacking in energy that we were left with a negative impression. Given these, she didn't seem "current" enough with trends to be effective in this particular role. Another candidate was responsive to our initial e-mail but couldn't schedule time for a phone interview until our process was nearly completed. Had we included this otherwise impressive candidate, our hiring decision would have been delayed by 2 weeks during a time when we needed to have a consultant hired, trained, and ready to begin working with clients.
>
> Ultimately, we hired a talented candidate who arranged to talk with us in the middle of her vacation. (We worked around her golf schedule.) She recognized our organization's needs, and we appreciated her flexibility.

The lessons here? When you are contacted by an organization offering a job you'd like to have, respond professionally and appropriately and in a timely manner. Recognize their timeline and accommodate their needs whenever possible. Top candidates have lost opportunities when they failed to respond as expected.

Types of Interviews

There are several types of interviews. The type of interview for which you have been contacted will dictate how you might best prepare for it. Here we describe the most common types.

Preliminary Interviews

These may be more informal and may take the guise of a friendly call from someone on the search committee. Often the caller will state that he or she simply "wants to clarify your experience with Gestalt therapy" or something similar. Remember, *any* contact you have with *any* individual representing the hiring organization may be part of the interview, so even a contact from an assistant in the human resources department could be one of the most important calls you ever take. A call *you* make to follow up on receipt of your application might even initiate a preliminary interview. Be prepared to have an in-depth conversation regarding your qualifications whenever the opportunity warrants.

Strategy

Recognize that if you receive a casual, possibly unexpected call, you are, indeed, being interviewed. Make sure you do most of the listening (take notes!), and let the caller control the flow and pace. Ask a few questions regarding the program, agency, or school. Do not make any critical comments, swear, chew gum, drink a beverage, or eat during this conversation (besides the danger of choking or coughing up liquids, eating or drinking while speaking on the phone sounds annoyingly rude). Before the call concludes, inquire about a formal interview.

Conference Interviews

At many conferences, prescreening interviews are conducted to allow both candidates and employers to determine whether a fit exists. At the American Counseling Association (ACA) annual conference, for example, faculty members will interview many potential counselor educators and make notes about each candidate's strengths and weaknesses to share with colleagues on their return to campus. Because these opportunities are often arranged by a third party (e.g., ACA Career Services), make certain you understand the process for registering, requesting interviews, scheduling, and communicating and meeting with interviewers. The organizers usually develop guidelines to ensure confidentiality and fairness to all candidates.

Strategy

In our experience, it's a definite advantage to see the people interviewing you and gauge their nonverbal expressions. Interviewers are also more likely to be favorable to candidates they have met in person versus simply spoken with on the phone or communicated with via e-mail. Dress as you would for any other interview, and have copies of your résumé or curriculum vitae (CV) available. Here, you also have the advantage of preparation time, so have four to six questions ready to ask the person or committee. As counseling professionals with lots of experience conducting interviews, we've observed that candidates with no questions demonstrate a lack of initiative. Remember, the committee is looking to see who they might wish to grant a formal interview, so be prepared to answer and ask relevant questions. When the interview is concluded, follow up with a thank-you letter accompanied by a CV and cover letter. (*Note:* E-mail is now an acceptable means by which to convey your respects.)

Job Fair Interviews

Job fair interviews are similar to conference interviews, but they are usually hosted by a university or consortium of universities in a specific geographic area. School districts that recruit out of their state and region will often use these for the purposes of screening potential teachers, counselors, and psychologists. Numerous potential counselors will be interviewed. Schools will select their finalists from the personnel they interviewed. As with conference interviews, make certain you've followed the proper procedures for registration because deadlines are often necessary to accommodate both employers and job seekers.

Strategy

The format will be very similar to the conference interview just discussed because an individual or a small panel will conduct screening interviews. Dress appropriately, bring your résumé, and have targeted questions you can ask the interviewers. Follow up with an additional copy of your résumé and a well-positioned cover letter based on the conversation you had with the school district's representatives.

Formal Telephone Interviews

Interviews by phone are used primarily to screen the potential list down to the finalists who are invited for on-site (in-person) interviews. For some global organizations, a phone interview (with or without the benefit of a Webcam) may be *the* interview. Depending on the nature of the job, virtual interviewing is commonplace for virtual work.

Strategy

Unlike the preliminary interview discussed earlier, this encounter is expected. Have your résumé or CV out because the committee may refer to it. Expect some 8–15 questions depending on the time frame. Sometimes search committees will stack phone interviews and have only 30 minutes per candidate, so be judicious, but thorough, in your answers. Some candidates we have worked with dress up for the phone interview because it helps put them in the interview mood. We suggest you do whatever helps you feel most confident—whether that is formal dress or sweats and slippers. Some career experts suggest you stand during the interview to walk off interview anxiety, although we suggest using whatever style feels most comfortable to you. Again, listen carefully, let the interviewer or panel control the process, and don't interrupt because it's considered rude. Have the standard 6–8 questions ready to ask the committee. Before the interview concludes, ask them about their process—specifically, when they expect to bring candidates on site. Follow up with a thank-you note to reinforce your strengths for the position and to add any additional insights on which you'd like to elaborate. (Again, e-mail is acceptable and quicker.)

On-Site (In-Person) Interviews

Congratulations! You have been invited to interview on site at the school, agency, or university. At this stage, you're one of the finalists for the position. The competition, at this point, will generally number between three and six finalists. If you travel a significant distance or if you're interviewing for a university position, it is very possible that you will have meetings scheduled over 2 to 3 days' time.

Strategy

From the time you initially meet with anyone connected with the school, agency, or counselor education program, you are "on," so if you've just landed after a long plane ride, consider popping into a gateside restroom to freshen up before meeting a search committee member at the baggage claim. Everything you say and do is subject to critique by the search committee (and search committees can be as capricious as a sorority during rush). Try to be as natural as you can under the circumstances.

One additional tip: When you are invited for an on-site interview that involves significant travel, be certain to ask how your expenses will be handled. Do not assume that your expenses are covered unless you have clarified this with the person who issues the invitation. The job search process is filled with horror stories of unreimbursed costs at applicants' expense. Don't assume, but be clear on reimbursement, and keep all receipts.

Preparing for Interviews

First, conduct a mental clearing of your perceptions and projections regarding the upcoming interview. It's natural and even desirable to be excited about the prospect of a new job. But because desire and "job fit" are different concepts, excitement must be tempered with caution. You don't really know what it would be like to do this job. The interview process is designed to help you explore the fit between you and the potential job.

Many spiritual traditions (Chodron, 1997) warn against overattachment. The bottom line is that it's best not to become too attached to a job before you have had an interview. In many cases, you may not have visited the agency, school, or college or even met the staff. Thus, we recommend you ground yourself in preparation and be prepared to take an objective look at your place of prospective employment.

(Amy jumping in here. . . .) I frequently compare interviewing with dating. You already know a little about the other party, and what you know, you are inclined to like. But until you've experienced that first date, you have a lot of questions. Just as you would not start planning a wedding until at least the most important of those questions are answered, you don't want to commit to one specific job until you've had an opportunity to find out more about the expectations and benefits.

As a counselor, you've certainly learned about empathy, and the interview process is one time when this knowledge can be put to practical, personal use.

As You Prepare to Interview, Put Yourself in the Position of Your Interviewers

- What knowledge, skills, or values are they seeking to add to their team?
- What are the greatest challenges the organization is currently facing or expects to face in the future?
- What would you bring to the organization that would enhance or complement their mission?

Just as job advertisements are helpful when you are structuring a cover letter, they should also be the basis of your interview preparation. Look at the details. Is there a job description available from the organization? It *is* appropriate to request this from the contact who extends the interview offer to you if it isn't already available online. Carefully read—and reread—the job description to ensure you haven't missed anything. (You might be surprised at how often job candidates seem to have missed a pertinent area of the position description.) What are the specific requirements of this position?

As you review the advertisement and job description, consider each point carefully. What specific skills and experience do you bring that will address that particular need? Have you had successes with specific programs or techniques that may be of interest to those who will interview you?

Check the organization's Web site. Do they have a published mission statement? How could you fit into that structure? Do you share the institution's vision? How? Can you enthusiastically support it, especially in the interview process? Be prepared to demonstrate your knowledge and how you complement the tenets of the institution's mission.

Make sure you have examined the school, clinic, or counselor education program's Web site and know the staff and their respective areas and specialties. If you are a counseling education applicant, is the current program accredited by the Council for Accreditation of Counseling and Related Educational Programs (CACREP)? Or does it have a timeline for achieving accreditation? Read and be able to address the mission statement of both the institution and the counselor education department. In our experience, many candidates get tripped up by ignoring the mission statement. Do not add your name to this infamous list!

Now, look at your application materials as an interviewer would. If you were interviewing yourself, what questions would your application materials elicit? What strengths do you see here? As you compare yourself with the job description, what are your weaknesses? Ask a faculty member or colleague to review the materials you submitted for recommendations on questions they would ask you if they were on the search committee.

Don't be overly concerned if you are missing some experience called for in the job advertisement. As we've discussed previously, this is a wish list, and if you have an invitation for an interview, you've impressed the search committee at least enough to be considered for the position. That said, you need to be able to address the weaknesses in your candidacy and respond to them with a clear strategy to overcome them.

Review our list of employer questions and have a friend, spouse, or someone ask you the questions and grade your responses. In addition, try to think of any other questions you might be asked.

Turn the Table Back to You

Many job seekers forget a key component in interviewing. You aren't just seeking to impress a search committee. You are attempting to find a professional home, one that fits you as well as you fit it. You, in effect, are interviewing everyone whom you meet within the organization as they interview you.

What questions do *you* want to have answered?

- Who will your colleagues be? Do you like them? Do you respect them?
- Who will your supervisor be? Do you like him or her?
- How does your potential supervisor get along with his or her supervisor? (Watch for rifts in the chain of command. You can notice rifts through caustic comments, body language, or a slip of the tongue by support staff, students, etc.)
- If you're interviewing for a vacancy, why did the last person leave?
- If you're being considered for a newly created position, who has been fulfilling most of these responsibilities? Is the interim counselor also applying for the position? Will he or she relinquish ownership if you take over? Is this position funded on a temporary basis, or has it been designated as part of the general budget?
- What are the components of the job?
- Are there unwritten rules that don't show up in the job description? (*Note:* You *will* need to be discreet to ferret out sensitive information.)
- Is there a budget for professional development support? How is this distributed?

Beyond the job and the institution, you may have additional considerations. Think about the questions you need to have answered regarding the nonwork side of your life. This is particularly important if relocation is involved.

- Is this a community in which I would like to live?
- Is appropriate housing available to me, and can I afford it?
- Are there opportunities for me (and my family, if this is a factor) to continue participation in the activities that I enjoy or that are important to me?
- If I have children, are the public schools successful? What are the private alternatives, and are they within my budget?

- If my job were eliminated at some point after I relocated to this area, would there be other employment opportunities? Would my accompanying partner (if applicable) be able to find meaningful work within a commutable distance?

Remember Some Communication Basics From Legend Dale Carnegie

1. Become genuinely interested in other people.
2. Smile.
3. Remember that a person's name is to that person the sweetest and most important sound in any language.
4. Be a good listener. Encourage others to talk about themselves.
5. Talk in terms of the other person's interests.
6. Make the other person feel important—and do it sincerely. (Carnegie, 1981, p. 112)

Questions to Be Prepared to Answer

Some of these questions are generic and could be asked with respect to any counseling position, whereas some are specific to agency, school, or academic counselor education positions. This is not a comprehensive list, but many of the questions we list may be asked in your interview. Be prepared to answer each of them.

It may be helpful to have an objective partner help you to rehearse answering these questions. If you feel that it's constructive, request that the person asking you the questions grade you on a scale ranging from 1 to 10, with 1 being *very poor*, 5 being *average*, and 10 being *outstanding*. Also, ask your practice interviewer whether she or he would hire you on the basis of your answers. If you are a graduate student, your institution's career center may have a practice interview program.

Videotaping your practice interview can provide you with the opportunity to watch nonverbal behaviors. Given that a lot of communication is nonverbal, we recommend you gauge whether your answers to interview questions and your nonverbal behavior are congruent.

Two quick points, before you check out the questions:

If you don't know the answer to a question, it's okay to say, "I don't know." This displays both honesty and lack of pretension. Besides, experienced search committees have heard lots of "B.S." answers. You want to sound authentic.

Bolles (2004) pressed the need to attend to the "50/50, 2-minute max" rule. This means you will listen half the time and ask questions half the time. The 2-minute maximum suggests that you keep your answers thorough but brief. The longer you talk, the greater the likelihood that search committee members will tune you out. Also, the longer you talk during an interview, the greater the likelihood that you will disclose something you would rather not disclose. (We can't tell you how often this latter issue occurs, much to the candidate's chagrin!)

1. *Why do you want this job?* This is a critical question, and potential employers will be very interested in your answer. You want the search committee or the individual interviewing you to believe this school, agency, or counselor education department is your primary focus and interest. Focus on employer needs: specifically, what you are able to contribute and where you see professional growth opportunities in research and so forth. Being able to tie your answer to the primary mission of the school, agency, or counselor education department or university is a good idea.

2. *Why are you considering leaving your present counseling or faculty position?* Be positive! Don't give the impression that you are running away from a bad situation—even if you are. A good answer may focus on specific elements of the opportunity that interest you and are not part of your current position.

3. *Tell me about yourself.* This is a *carpe diem* moment. We know of professional outplacement firms who encourage clients to develop a "60-second commercial" or an "elevator speech." Weave your personal and professional story—briefly—into something related to why you would be a good fit for the job. Because you want to sound authentic, practice your answer with a friend, colleague, or career counselor and have him or her grade you on your genuineness. Practicing to be authentic may sound contrived, but it is a wise thing to do.

4. *What special training or skills can you offer?* Provide details that either directly respond to specific job responsibilities that have been advertised or discuss a "value-added" skill that might entice the employer to recognize that you have attributes beyond the scope of what the organization is seeking. For example, if you are a certified mediator, work that information into the interview.

5. *What's your experience in this area of counseling?* If you are a young counseling graduate student, highlight your practicum and internship. If you have related experience—say, working as a college resident advisor, summer camp counselor, or case manager at a human service agency—weave that into your answer.

6. *Could you describe your strengths and weaknesses?* Everyone has weaknesses, and you are no exception. The classic (and overused) answer is "I tend to be a perfectionist, never satisfied with my own performance." Even noncounselor types recognize that *this* candidate is headed for serious trouble! Be genuine, but use discretion. Try to relate a weakness that can also be a strength. (Amy here: My favorite answer to this question came from a participant in an outplacement workshop I was conducting a couple of years ago. The job seeker said in response to this practice question, "Well, I'm not 18 anymore. But then again, I'm not 18 anymore!" With this answer, she effectively addressed her own maturity in the workplace and added some levity to the process. Shannon here: Another approach to the "weakness" question is to introduce an area you have improved on, for example, "In the past, an area needing

improvement would have been my lack of familiarity with addictions counseling. In the past year, however, I have completed a professional certificate in addictions counseling and assessment.")

7. *If offered this position, how long could you see yourself working here?* In most cases, it's best not to give a specific length of time. Instead, say something such as "As long as I have fresh challenges and opportunities, I could see myself working here for the foreseeable future."

8. *What theoretical approach to counseling do you work from? Why?* All counselors on the job search must be able to articulate whether their approach to counseling is client centered, cognitive–behavioral, solution focused, integrated framework, and so on. Applicants who cannot answer this question concisely are unlikely to be offered the job.

9. *How do you handle conflict?* The individual answers will vary here. Recognize that this is a commonly asked question, and be prepared to answer it. Be judicious with your answer, but also be real. A possible response to this question might be something like

> I work to get myself calm and then review what I believe are the main points of disagreement, then seek out the other party from the standpoint of trying to understand their point of view. If we cannot come to some agreement ourselves, perhaps getting a colleague or supervisor to mediate might be a good idea.

10. *What theoretical supervisory approach do you work from?* This question is primarily for counselor education and clinical supervisory applicants; responses may be, for example, social–constructivist, psychodynamic, and so forth.

11. *What are your professional goals? Or, more specifically, regarding your career, where would you like to be in 10 years?* This is another question that will be candidate specific. You will want to demonstrate in your answer that you are forward thinking but also recognize the need for flexibility as opportunities emerge.

12. *Who has been most influential in your life and why?* This is a type of get-to-know-you question. Several people may have been influential. As you prepare for your interview, consider how you would answer this question. It's one of those that isn't *always* asked, but if it is, it's an easy one to stumble on.

13. *What's your experience in working with at-risk youth?* This and other questions like it may be directed at specific counseling experiences. It might not always be at-risk youth. It could be undecided majors or postpartum depression. Be prepared to discuss the special populations with which you have worked.

14. *What if a teacher asks for information about a student you have been counseling? Do you give the information to her?* This question falls into the behavioral approach to interviewing, which is becoming more popular because it addresses the need to review candidates in an objective manner. Expect other "What would you do if . . . ?" questions and try to frame them in a situation–task–approach–results response.

15. *Regarding research, what's your specialty area?* This is a question more commonly targeted to counselor education applicants, but be ready to discuss anything that is on your résumé or CV. If you are applying for an academic position, you should be able to articulate your research interests and experience. Also, before your interview, check out the department's Web site to get a sense of the current faculty's research. An ability to demonstrate how your scholarly interests match up with theirs is very important. Also, be able to illustrate that you bring something a little different to the research table.

16. *Why were you fired (if fired) or why did you leave your last job?* Careful here. Be positive, but truthful. If you were terminated for cause, you need to be up-front about that and then quickly outline your correction or success since being fired. Emphasize that you have learned from this painful experience, and explain how you have grown from it. Remember, the world is full of successful people who have been fired from previous jobs. In today's employment world, it's possible someone interviewing you may have been fired and could thus empathize with you.

17. *What salary would you expect to receive?* Always respond, "Somewhere in the advertised range" or "something reflecting my training and experience." *Never state a dollar amount until you receive an offer.*

18. *What did you like about our school, clinic, or counselor education program that interested you enough to apply for the job?* This is a critical question. The answer the interviewing committee wants to hear involves the candidate's illustrating an in-depth knowledge of the agency, school, or counselor education program; its mission, goals, or treatment or educational approach; dedicated staff here at the school, agency, or counselor education department; and so forth. Be brief, but show you have done your homework.

19. *What do you see as the pressing issues in the field for the next decade?* This question is designed to see how well you understand the profession, and it is particularly critical for those who are interviewing for positions as counselor educators. Your critics are looking to see if you are relevant! The pressing issues are debatable, so be prepared to support what you mention, for example, "I believe multicultural competence is critical because of growing immigrant and cultural populations," "I believe a critical issue is Web-based counselor education," or "I see the international counseling movement as the biggest potential issue," and so forth.

20. *What professional counseling organizations do you hold membership in?* As we have said before, if you do not have a current membership in the ACA, American School Counselor Association (ASCA), American Mental Health Counselors Association (AMHCA), or a pertinent organization, get one immediately! Counselors with professional memberships demonstrate a greater commitment to the counseling field than those who lack such membership.

21. *How have you or would you support multiculturalism?* Multiculturalism is the number one issue in today's counseling field. Be ready to address how you support multiculturalism and include specific examples. For

example, serving on the school district's Diversity Task Force or the college's Committee on the Status of Women is concrete proof.

22. *What additional or special training do you have?* Some examples are trauma counseling, play therapy, dialectical behavioral therapy, mediation, and so forth. Furthermore, if you hold specialized training, you may be able to provide in-house training for counselors, teachers, administration, and colleagues. Specialized training is valuable.

23. *What do you know about the mission of the university, school, or agency, and how would the mission guide you in this job?* We recommend you be prepared to answer this question intelligently. Most mission statements are "big picture" in description and address, for example, "creating a more just society" or "providing opportunities for underrepresented persons." Be prepared to explain how you fit with the mission statement and cite specific examples.

24. *Why should we hire you?* All interviews are an attempt to address this key question. Such a question usually comes last, if at all. Try to focus on employer needs and your qualifications and ability to address them. You also want to sound confident, although not cocky, in your answer. Here's one possible answer:

> I believe myself to be the best candidate for the school counseling position because I have spent the past 2 [or 4, or 5, etc.] years working in a P–12 setting. I also have experience in vocational and academic counseling and art therapy and am passionate about student well-being and achievement. I have already articulated my ideas about educational programming during the interview and would be excited about implementing them here at Salem High School. Hire me as a school counselor, and I'll make you very happy you did.

25. *Do you have any questions for me (us)?* Of course you do! This is your opportunity to take control of the interview, and failure to do so may hurt your candidacy. Shannon cringes (inwardly) when he observes candidates who state with aplomb, "I have no questions." This statement implies that the candidate did not do her or his homework or perhaps even a lack of interest. You always need to have questions to ask, even if they have already been answered outside the formal interview room. We suggest you make a list of questions to ask based on your thorough study of the school, agency, treatment center, hospital, or counselor education department. We have listed some sample questions later. Naturally, you'll probably have some of your own as well.

Inappropriate Questions

Occasionally in the course of an interview, questions may be asked that are generally deemed inappropriate. Often, these questions are asked by inexperienced interviewers who generally mean no harm but may be attempting to establish rapport with you and get to know you as a person. They *should* know better, but they don't always. And, of course, some interviewers ask questions they know to be inappropriate.

For university positions, most public and private universities have an Equal Employment Opportunity Commission (EEOC) statement that pledges that they will not discriminate on the basis of race, gender, creed, or national origin, and many add sexual orientation to this list. A handful of private institutions do not accept government funds (e.g., federal financial aid for students) and are not subject to EEOC governance.

Questions dealing with any of the EEOC protected classifications are off limits unless there are circumstances in which they qualify as a bona fide occupational qualification. An example would be a private, Christian college that requires a statement of faith consistent with the mission of the institution.

Examples of inappropriate questions include

- "Are you married?" or "Do you have children?"
- "What is your religion?"
- "What is your sexual orientation?"
- "Which political party do you belong to?"

(I [Shannon] was once a candidate at an interview during which I was questioned about my political affiliation, religion, and marital status. Despite being fresh out of a graduate school and nearly broke, I decided I wasn't *that* desperate for a job!)

The professional way to respond to illegal or inappropriate questions is to be tactful and ask clarification questions:

Example of inappropriate question: "Are you married?"

Sample answer: "How does that question relate to the job?" or "Why is this important to know?" You might also use humor in your response, especially if you have no reason to believe ill intent exists. "Hmmm . . . I don't think the interview police allow that question. Why do you ask?" This type of response is nonconfrontational and gives your interviewer an opportunity to save face.

Given that the interview is the time during which both parties are generally on their best behavior, inappropriate questions would rightfully lead a candidate to wonder about the school, agency, or counselor education program's *worst* behavior! You do need a job; you don't need a job where the professional dispositions are illegal, unethical, or otherwise inappropriate because this will only create greater stress for you should you accept a job at a school, agency, or counselor education department that is so ethically challenged.

If you *are* asked one of these inappropriate questions or something along these lines and you have reason to believe that malice was intended, you may want to consider whether this is the type of school, agency, or institution you would want to represent. It's understandable you want a job, but do you want *any* job? We also recommend that if you are asked inappropriate questions, you may, after the search process is concluded, consider contacting the appropriate person in the agency, school, or institution and informing them of your experience. Highly paid administrators should be aware of what the people they supervise are doing. If the affluent administrator was the problem, she or he has a board of directors who should be interested in your experiences. If the board is not interested in such egregious behavior, you don't want to work there anyway. (And you don't want your friends or colleagues working there either!)

Questions You Might Ask the Search Committee

1. What preferred qualities or experience would you like in a new colleague?
2. What do (each of) you like about working at this school, clinic, or counselor education program?
3. What challenges are you facing? (Or target the specific audience: "What challenges is this school counseling department facing?")
4. Why did the last counselor or counselor educator leave?
5. Have you experienced a downsizing or staffing increase recently?
6. Is there a budget for travel to conferences or continuing education (schools and clinics)? If so, what's the amount, and how is it distributed?
7. What courses would I be teaching (counselor education)?
8. What goals has your department, school counseling center, or agency set? (*Note:* If the answer is none, you should be concerned.)
9. What special programs might I be offering (e.g., recovery groups, peer helping groups, preparing for college groups)?
10. What priorities would you have for me?
11. Do you offer a mentoring program for new counselors or counselor educators?
12. What are you most proud of about your school, agency, or counselor education program?
13. When do you anticipate making a decision regarding this position?
14. If I were to be selected for this position, what type of financial support is available for relocation costs(if relevant)?

What *Not* to Ask

There's an old saying among executive recruiters: "He who speaks money first loses." If money and benefits are discussed during your interview, be certain that you are not the one who initiates the discussion. You are there to learn about the *job*, and although the compensation package is a criterion that you will consider, you do not want to give the impression that this is your foremost concern.

With that in mind, you do want to be able to respond to questions about your salary expectations. For counselor education professors and student affairs staff, the *Chronicle of Higher Education* publishes an annual almanac that can be helpful in identifying appropriate salary ranges for various positions. You may also want to consult a cost-of-living calculator (an Internet search will yield a number of hits) to determine the value of the salary in the target location compared with the local economy with which you are already familiar.

If the topic of compensation comes up, you want to first clarify the range of salary that is budgeted for the position if it hasn't already been communicated. Respond with a range that you would be willing to accept. If your range is slightly higher than the posted range, be prepared to identify value-added skills that would place you at the top end of the pay scale. Many factors, including the overall economy, may influence whether there is room for negotiation in salary. Be aware that in tough economic times, you'll have more success in negotiating nonmonetary elements of the compensation package.

Preparing Your Wardrobe for Interviews

With "business casual" reigning in some of even the most conservative boardrooms these days, there's no doubt that standards for professional dress have relaxed quite a bit over the past 25 years. But even in this era of "less is more," interviewing still stands as one of the occasions when it is most appropriate to wear a suit or at least a "suit look." Proper attire—and improper attire—can swing an interview one direction or another. First impressions made within the opening minutes of an interview can be lasting. In most cases, play it conservative. (*Note:* For Shannon, dress may be the *one* area of his life in which he is a conservative!)

Dress in accordance with interviews in the counseling field. Counseling professionals do not typically dress in the same manner as accountants. Still, a general guideline is to dress "up" rather than "down." After all, you are entering a profession in which you are entrusted with the health and well-being of human beings.

For women, that means a coordinating jacket and skirt or well-tailored pants, accessorized with an appropriate blouse, hosiery, and shoes. Jewelry and other accessories should complement your ensemble and your personality, but guard against wearing anything that is overpowering and distracting. (You don't want the search committee to be more interested in your accessories than they are in you!) Be conservative with makeup and perfume because too much of either can be overpowering and distracting, as well.

Male candidates would be best served by wearing a sports coat, tie, and slacks. If fragrance is worn at all, it should be very light. Socks are an absolute requirement, as are sensible, although polished, dress shoes.

Use of deodorants should go without saying, especially because you may be perspiring. Mouthwash is recommended, as are breath mints tucked into a pocket or briefcase. Empty your pockets of anything that might jingle.

Hair styles for counselors generally do not correspond to IBM standards, but make sure that however you wear your hair, it's neat. Avoid frayed coats, collars, and any clothing that seems unkempt, ragged, dirty, or flamboyant. Although a job interview isn't a fashion show, you should check to see that colors and patterns match.

Before leaving for the interview, look at yourself in the mirror and ask, "Would I hire this person for the job?"

This little ditty may help you with appropriate interview presence:

Navy blue—trite, but true,
Rings on hands—no more than two.
Hair is neat, nails trimmed,
Shoes are polished—You can win!

Check your look out in a mirror,
And don't forget—Smile, dear!
Stand up straight, chin held high.
Shake hands firmly with a friendly "Hi!"

The Execution

Once you've adequately prepared for an interview, you're ready to execute it. (And if you haven't prepared, you may feel as though you're about to *be* executed.) We promise you that once you recognize that the best interviews are simple conversations among professional colleagues, you will stop fearing and eventually enjoy them.

Your Arrival

Plan to arrive 10 to 15 minutes early. If you are driving yourself, make certain to allow plenty of time for traffic and weather-related slowdowns. If your interview is on a college campus (or, similarly, a metropolitan area with remote parking) and you are driving yourself, allow time to park in a designated parking area and walk to the appointed area. You'll want to familiarize yourself with the campus map and arm yourself with a cell phone and telephone numbers for search committee members and the departmental administrator in case you need directions.

Once in the correct building, duck into a restroom to freshen up and check your appearance one last time before reporting for your interview. Realize that as soon as you leave your vehicle, you're "on." (If you are not already accustomed to treating everyone you encounter with respect and kindness, this may be a very good habit to begin practicing now, before you even start interviewing.) Anyone you encounter from the time your feet hit the pavement should be regarded as a possible interviewer.

First Impressions

You may recall reading in a textbook or hearing from your professor that hiring decisions are made in the first 3 to 5 minutes of an interview. This suggests the interviewer or search committee is not simply looking at your résumé or CV but internally asking some basic questions:

- Do I like Jim?
- Will Sylvia fit in with our school, agency, or department?
- Is Steve honest?
- Would I want Lucia as a colleague?

These types of questions are probably going through the interviewers' minds not only in those first few critical minutes, but also as they review the performance of candidates they have interviewed as their decision-making process concludes.

Simple things like presenting a firm (but not *too* firm) handshake, maintaining eye contact, and having good posture provide nonverbal input to support a positive first impression. A genuine smile will help to put others at ease, as well.

What Happens in an Interview?

In each interview session, at least a few minutes will be devoted to introductions. (This is where your "Tell me about yourself" answer will come in to play. As previously noted, be prepared to give a synopsis of your background. For interest, you may want to include some information that isn't on your résumé.) As others introduce themselves, take note of their names and positions. This task is made easier if you're already familiar with the organizational chart.

Often, the next phase of the interview will focus on the job requirements. There may be specific questions about your experience with and understanding of particular issues. If this is a behavioral interview, which is not very typical in higher education but is a possibility because this type of interview is growing in popularity, you may not have much interaction with the panel of interviewers, who may be taking many notes and scoring your responses. (A behavioral interview is usually a series of questions that are asked of all candidates for a specific position. The questions are designed to determine how the candidate has behaved in the past in given situations or how he or she describes what behavior she or he would exhibit at present or in the future.) Once the interviewer or interview panel has asked all of their questions of you, they'll invite your questions.

Campus Interview

Higher education is respected (or to some, *notorious*) for searching for consensus. As a result, on-campus interviews are often lengthy affairs, providing opportunities for multiple parties to meet candidates and share their assessments. This is particularly true if the position for which you are interviewing is a faculty position or a management-level student affairs position, such as director of counseling. Here is an example of an interview schedule for a candidate for director of a counseling center at an unnamed university:

Day 1
- Arrive at the airport, where you are met by one or more members of the search committee.
- Check in to the hotel where you will be staying.
- Meet members of the search committee for an "informal" dinner.

Day 2
- Meet the chair of the search committee for breakfast meeting.
- Interview with the entire search committee.
- Meet with the staff of the department (e.g., University Counseling Center) that you would be joining.
- Have lunch with a group of selected student leaders.

- Make a presentation to interested members of the university community. (You may be asked to give a PowerPoint presentation or answer questions from the audience.)
- Meet with the department chair.
- Go back to the hotel to rest and freshen up.
- Have dinner with selected members of the search committee.

Day 3
- Have a breakfast meeting with the vice president or provost.
- Meet with faculty or administrators from other departments (e.g., counselor education, counseling, or education).
- Meet with human resources representative.
- Return to the airport, escorted by member of search committee.

If you are invited for a campus interview, you'll typically be apprised of your schedule ahead of time. If, for some reason, you are not scheduled to have an informal session with students, or with any other group you would like to see represented, you can request it, particularly if you believe that this interaction would provide you with insight into the campus community.

You can usually count on a tour of the campus at some point during your interview, and possibly a tour of the surrounding community. We know of at least one case in which a colleague being interviewed for a high-level administrative position was treated to a tour of the city by the mayor to ensure good town–gown relations.

Sometimes, the university will arrange for time with a realtor, particularly if relocation on acceptance would be in order. If you have an accompanying partner, you might gain insight into his or her employment opportunities during a meeting with a representative from HR or from the University Career Center.

As you can imagine, this is a whole lot of "on" time, and if you tend to be an introvert, you will need to prepare yourself mentally for this grueling interviewing program.

Appropriate Behavior and Etiquette

There's no need to pull out Amy Vanderbilt's famed book, although there are some basic standards of behavior to observe.

- *Always be on time for your interview.* In fact, show up 7 to 10 minutes early to show interest and also to mentally prepare for the interview. Showing up unusually early may suggest overanxiousness. Showing up late may cost you the job.
- *Come to the interview alone.* Do not bring your partner or spouse, best friend, or roommate. Arriving at an interview accompanied by others suggests that you may do this if hired. Incidentally, Shannon can recall odd incidents such as one in which an applicant brought his mother to the interview. Because she knew him better than anyone, he asked her to come along in the event the panel decided to ask her some questions. (He was not offered the job.)

- *Make a strong connection with the interviewer or panel.* When the interview begins, try to get the search committee members' first names committed to memory and occasionally use their names to refer to critical points during the interview process. Use the names or titles by which committee members introduced themselves. For example, don't use the familiar *Bobby* for Robert, and if search committee members refer to themselves as *Doctor, Ms.,* or *Mr.,* refer to them by that title.
- *Let the search committee members control the flow of the interview.* When questions are asked, use the 30-second rule and don't take longer than that to answer a question (Bolles, 2007). In Shannon's experience, faculty are more likely than most counselors to be long-winded. In one interview Shannon sat in on, one faculty candidate took 45 minutes on one question! (He was not offered the job.) If you are asked a question and don't know the answer, simply reply, "I don't know." Uttering these three simple words indicates both honesty and proper humility—after all, no one has all the answers and nobody likes working with a know-it-all. Seasoned search committee members have developed a reliable B.S. meter and will know when a candidate is trying to bluff his or her way through an answer. Finally, have the usual 10 to 15 questions ready to query the search committee. After all, given that this could be a significant change in geography and responsibility, you should be interviewing them as well.

The search committee may treat you to lunch or dinner. If so, there are some simple behavioral guidelines to follow:

- Eat slowly and carefully because poor table manners will reflect poorly on you and might undermine your candidacy. Do not talk with your mouth full (as your mother may have instructed you long ago). Unless others order alcohol, refrain from doing so.
- If you do order a beer or glass of wine, have only one drink, and nurse it. Years ago, Shannon was on a search committee that took a candidate to dinner. The candidate, who up until that time was a strong favorite to receive a job offer, proceeded to down a handful of drinks. This candidate's overindulgence effectively eliminated him from serious consideration!
- In addition to going light on the sauce, be wary about letting down too much at the meal. Do not make critical comments about past employers, or get into political or religious discussions because you are certain to offend someone. Naturally, you have the right to voice criticisms and promote the political, social, and spiritual values of your choice—but wait until after you have taken the job before you do.
- If dessert is offered, look to the rest of your party before accepting or declining. If it appears that others may be interested in indulging and you don't care to do so, order a coffee. This extends the time available for conversation, particularly if things are going well. (And if a potential colleague asks whether you'd be interested in sharing a dessert,

this could be a good sign that he or she is already thinking of you as part of the team.)

- When the meal is over, thank the committee members for the outing, and if this is the parting moment, thank them for the opportunity to interview for the job. Politely inquire as to when you might hear a final decision on the job.
- Overall, keep in mind that completing your meal is not the objective of this dinner. Save the "Clean Plate Club" for family meals, and recognize that your primary objective is positive social interaction with prospective colleagues.

Following Up After the Interview

When you return home, send the search committee a thank-you card or an e-mail thanking them for the interview. Personalizing correspondence with each committee member by identifying and addressing their specific areas of interest can enhance your candidacy. We guarantee that committee members will compare their perceptions of you, and this may include your written correspondence.

Photocopy all receipts for reimbursement. We have heard too many stories of job candidates not being reimbursed fully because of lost receipts. In one case, the head of the search committee refused to reimburse a candidate for the hotel, meals, and gas money, stating that he had received no receipts. Fortunately, the candidate had back-up copies. Still, the head of the search committee refused to reimburse the candidate. Finally, after almost 6 months, the candidate (who had not been offered the job) sent the copied receipts to the search committee chair's supervisor. The candidate was reimbursed fully and received a written apology from the search chair's supervisor!

If You Don't Receive an Offer

Ouch! We know it hurts to be rejected. If this was a job you wanted or were counting on, the disappointment will certainly be greater than if you were just going through the interview for practice. Either way, you need to cross this one off the list, learn from the process, and apply the knowledge you have gained to the next interview. Dealing with job rejection and the subsequent emotions are covered in detail in chapter 5.

There are some basic issues and questions to entertain when you are rejected for a job. Naturally, feedback from the search committee would be most helpful, but in this litigious age such feedback is very unlikely. Still, we recommend that you ask the search committee chair (or whomever contacted you), "Was there anything I could have done differently that would have made a difference?" Most especially, we recommend you engage in a process of self-reflection:

- Remember, everyone has experienced job rejection. (Yes, everyone— including the authors of this venerable text!) Ask, "What lessons did I gain from the experience?"
- What did I do well during the interview process?
- What could I improve on next time?

If you have continued interest in a position, even though you have been notified that you were not the selected candidate, you might consider sending a letter to the chair of the search committee, thanking him or her for the opportunity to interview and expressing your continued interest if other positions open at a later time. Occasionally, the original selection falls through, and if another favored candidate is still available, the committee may extend an offer to a second choice without reopening the search.

Handling a Job Offer

Wow, you have a job offer! Congratulations! A job offer is always a big deal even if it is for a job you don't want.

When you receive an offer, it may be tempting to accept on the spot, particularly if you're already visualizing your name on the door of the office you just saw. Be aware, though, that if you accept immediately, you lose any leverage you have to review the entire compensation package and negotiate more favorable terms.

Certainly, you should express excitement at being offered the opportunity, and you may agree, in principle, that you are inclined to accept, but ask for the offer—in writing—and request any supplemental information (such as an employee handbook or other materials that provide details regarding benefits) that you will need to evaluate the specifics for your employment.

Go through the decision-making process carefully. We recommend that you ask for a few days to think the offer over and weigh the pros and cons objectively. Even if this is your dream job and you are absolutely certain you want it, take a few days to discuss the matter with your spouse or partner or with a trusted confidant who can help you to be objective. This also gives you time to assess what you would need to make the transition. There are many issues to consider:

- What changes would accepting this job entail?
- What expenses would I incur by accepting the job (e.g., moving expenses, selling or buying a home, and uprooting children from a school and friends)?
- What would I be gaining in accepting this job?
- What would I be giving up by accepting this job?

Of course, some jobs bring fewer changes than others. If you accept a counseling position that does not require relocation or one in the agency you are currently at with people you already know and familiar surroundings, the change may not seem so daunting. If, however, the job would necessitate your moving cross country, uprooting your family, and paying thousands of dollars to move your belongings, possibly to an area with a higher cost of living, then you have much to consider. Weigh the pros and cons of the job carefully before arriving at a decision.

A simple counseling technique may be helpful in assessing the benefits and drawbacks to accepting a position. Split a sheet of paper in half by drawing a line down the center. Label the left half *Pro* and the right half *Con*.

Then list both pros and cons. Naturally, you want the Pro list to far outnumber the Con list. If the Pro list is significantly longer, making a decision may be easy. If, however, the lists are of near-equal length or the con list is longer, this gives you something to think about before accepting the offer.

Pro	*Con*
1. More money	1. More stress
2. A counseling job	2. Requires moving across the United States
3. More rewarding than current job	3. Expensive relocation
4. Better salary	4. Far from friends and family
5. More desirable area	5. My spouse would need a job.
6. It's a good offer.	6. I'll get other offers.
7. The job offers potential for promotion.	
8. I like the colleagues who interviewed me.	
9. I'm excited about the positive changes.	
10. Closer to family	

In this case, the pros slightly outnumbered the cons, although there are significant cons. The candidate would likely have a difficult decision to make. Fortunately, counseling is a growing profession (U.S. Department of Labor, 2008), and the odds are very good that there will be other offers.

A complication in the process may occur if a "deal breaker" shows up in the con column, even if the pro column is lengthy. Possible "knockout" factors might include a location to which a spouse refuses to relocate or where she or he would not be able to gain employment or a compensation package that will not cover your basic needs. One respected colleague recently turned down his dream job because accepting it would have been a huge financial step backward. Everything else about the job was perfect: desirable location, colleagues that he was quite eager to work with, good teaching load, and excellent research support. But when he did the math and requested compensation that would have, in effect, been a lateral move for him, accounting for cost-of-living disparities, the university could not meet his needs, and he had to walk away.

Some readers will be in the enviable position of entertaining multiple offers at the same time. If you are one of the counselors fortunate enough to have such a problem, carefully compare the offers. What is the salary differential? How do the health plans compare? Does one necessitate a more distant move? Does one have more potential for growth? Has one potential employer had difficulty retaining its hires? If so, why? Which job do you really want the most? Which job is in a more desirable location? Make a pro–con list like the preceding one and tease out which offer is best for you and your family. Always remember this pearl of wisdom: *A higher paying job is not necessarily a better one.*

Decision Tree: Making and Evaluating the Decision

Still wondering what decision to make? Here's a sample decision tree you might use for clarification. Continue down the list of questions until you get to a "no." A "no" answer would suggest that you seriously consider whether accepting this job is a healthy decision.

- *Step 1:* Do I want the job? Yes? No?
- *Step 2:* Does this job fit my or my family's needs regarding challenge, security, and stability? Yes? No?
- *Step 3:* If this necessitates a move, would I/my family be willing to relocate? Would the relocation cause a long-term disruption in our lives? Yes? No?
- *Step 4:* Do I feel confident committing to this job for 3 to 5 years? Yes? No?
- *Step 5:* Do the pros of this job outweigh the cons? Yes? No?
- If "Yes," do the pros *significantly* outweigh the cons?

If You Reject an Offer

Be professional. Thank the search committee chair for his or her time and for the opportunity. If you are accepting a position at another university, you may want to share this information, but you are certainly under no obligation to do so. If you regard the individuals you met during your interview experience as professional colleagues, then take the opportunity to contact them personally to let them know of your decision and to express your desire to keep in touch with them.

If the reason for your turning down an offer relates to improprieties in the interview process, you may want to describe your experience to the chief human resources officer of the institution. Be careful, though. You do not want to burn bridges. If you level charges of impropriety, be certain of your facts. Don't impugn anyone's professional reputation over petty misunderstandings, or your own reputation could be at risk.

If You Have Decided to Negotiate the Offer

Before you dive in, recognize that if you're going to negotiate, you should proceed gently and with some caution. This is not professional sports or the Fortune 500 sector, and offers have been pulled from candidates whose efforts have been regarded as overly aggressive.

Anyone extending a job offer understands that a savvy candidate may attempt to negotiate the best terms possible. Many people, and this may be especially true of counselors, or at least young counselors straight out of graduate school, are uncomfortable with negotiation. We suggest you determine what you need to accept the job, then practice negotiating with a friend, family member, or, naturally, with a career counselor.

The type of position (entry-level counselor or assistant professor vs. clinical director or department chair) will determine how much latitude is given in negotiation. Regardless, here are some guidelines to consider in the negotiation process:

- In many cases, a specific salary is not posted. A salary range is more common, and this implies room for negotiation. (*Note:* There's always some room for negotiation, although salary may not be the most negotiable item.) How far up the salary range you can negotiate depends on your experience, publications, how much they want you, and your own ability to negotiate.
- Beyond salary, what are the other negotiables? Does accepting the job necessitate a costly move? If so, how much financial assistance will the employer provide for the move? Are you a dual-income family? What job prospects does the area offer for your spouse or partner? Can the employer assist with finding your spouse or partner a job? If it's a university position, does the institution offer opportunities for dual-career couples?
- How good are the benefits? What does the health plan include? What retirement plan is offered? What is the typical delay for implementation of these plans? Can that be negotiated? A word to young counselors reading this book: Although health care plans and retirement may seem less "sexy" than salary, in a few years they will be even more important than salary, especially if you have children or develop health problems.
- How many vacation days do you receive? How many sick days? Do you have a previously scheduled trip for which you need to negotiate time off (with or without pay)?
- What type of annual salary or merit increase is offered? Will you start on a probationary period? When will you have your first evaluation?
- What opportunity is there for advancement? For counselor educators, when would you go up for tenure? After 5 years? After 7 years? Also, exactly what are the benchmarks for achieving tenure? For school counselors in districts that offer tenure, when would you be eligible? Would your tenure be with the administrative or teaching faculty group?

You get the idea. Make a list of what you need to accept the position, then practice negotiating before you contact the employer. Also understand that you will not get everything you want even if the employer wants you and you are skilled at negotiation.

Keep the following in mind as you negotiate:

- *You must be a cost-effective hire.* Generally, this means putting in 3 to 5 years of employment.
- *Your compensation usually relates to your level of responsibility.* Would you be a beginning counselor or a manager? An assistant professor or department chair?
- *Few salaries or salary ranges are chiseled in stone.* Schools, agencies, or counselor education departments that advertise a starting salary of $36,000, for example, are usually willing to go at least a little higher than what's advertised. Recognize, however, that because counselors mostly work for nonprofit agencies or schools, the negotiable range is

not like it is in the business world, particularly during times of economic turbulence when not-for-profits are particularly vulnerable to volatility in market fluctuations

- *Once you agree to a package, get the agreement in writing before accepting the job.* You do not want to be in the uncomfortable position of accepting a job and potentially moving a long distance only to find out what you were promised does not materialize. From our collective 30 years experience in the field, bait-and-switch is a far too common experience for people changing jobs.

Accepting a Job

Your new employer expects you to be enthusiastic when you accept an employment offer. Generally, you will accept twice: first, verbally, and then formally, in writing.

In your written acceptance of the job offer, provide details of what you are accepting, including the job title, start date, and specifics of the compensation package, especially any exceptions from normal policy that you negotiated. Express your enthusiasm and excitement to be joining the organization because this will set the tone for your first weeks in your new role.

Don't feel that you are professionally deficient if you receive only one offer. If it is the right offer and you are able to practice your craft in a desirable environment with colleagues you respect, then you should be pleased. Likewise, many professionals accept offers without negotiating any fine points and have happy, long-term careers.

Congratulations on successfully completing this phase. Now the real work begins!

Chapter

5

Rejection: Dealing With and Working Through Disappointment

On your career journey, you will occasionally encounter a few bumps in the road. Although setbacks during the job search process are natural and to be expected, the reality of actually experiencing job rejection (or, along similar lines, being fired) can be very stressful. Clearly, career rejection and disappointment isn't limited to that found during a job search, although difficulty in landing viable employment can lead to depression. In our experience, we have found that one limitation of most job search manuals is that little attention was paid to job search failure. Naturally, job search texts want to focus on and prepare you for success. We have attempted to do the same thing by providing our ideas, training, and expertise. Yet, because job rejection can be such a disappointing (and at times emotionally devastating) experience, we believed an entire chapter was needed to address ways to combat job search disappointment.

Downsizing, right-sizing, and market response to tough economies often result in job loss. Although many reading this book may be reacting to a rejection for a job they were pursuing, others may be beginning a job search as the result of losing a job. Recognizing the rejection and dealing with the ensuing emotional roller coaster is crucial to moving on and moving up. Still, because much of the focus of our text involves interviewing, we begin by examining how to deal with job rejection.

So . . . maybe you have just suffered a setback in your job search. That dream job you applied and interviewed for—the one you were sure to get—didn't materialize. Perhaps you had a great interview experience where the search committee or director seemed to hang on your every word. (Or so you believed.) You left the interview convinced you would soon be getting a call from the school principal, agency manager, vice chancellor of student affairs, or dean of the college in which the counselor education program was located offering you the job. Maybe you were so confident you even scripted out how you would negotiate your salary. Puffed with hubris and with your future as bright as August sunshine, everything in your vocational heaven seemed in place. Then, with a stilted phone call, form letter, or e-mail, poof—your dream burst into flames of anguish.

Or . . . Maybe the counseling agency who hired you to develop a program from the ground up, the job you take such pride in, just notified you that they can no longer afford to keep you on the payroll because of deep budget cuts. Dazed and confused by this unforeseen blow, you must now figure out how to replace that income.

Or . . . The promotion to director of the school counseling services that you thought was in the bag, the one that seemed written for you, didn't materialize. Worse still, it was given to a colleague you don't like. You're not out a job, but you feel less secure than before. Humbled and angry, you retreat to lick your wounds.

These examples are representative of experiences of job seekers worldwide. Frequently, the anticipated and expected fail to materialize, and the applicant is left empty handed and disappointed. We recommend you not beat yourself up because job rejection is as common as job success. In fact, every successful counselor, counselor educator, counseling supervisor, and career counselor has experienced job rejection and career disappointment. In many ways, job rejection may be even more common than success! In Shannon's own career, this has often been true (Hodges, 2001).

The critical factor for job seekers to acknowledge is that you *will* have failures. But job rejection means you are actively trying to land a job by networking with friends and setting up informational interviews, attending job fairs, examining the local or regional newspaper and publications such as *Counseling Today* and the *Chronicle of Higher Education*, and working with the campus career center or one of the federally funded employment training programs in your area, and much more.

Yes, you will have failures, but staying active and continuing to challenge disappointment makes it more likely that you will eventually experience job success. Now, because this chapter is devoted to job rejection, let's take a look at a well-known model borrowed from a famous researcher on grief and recovery, Elisabeth Kübler-Ross.

Stages of Job Rejection Grief (or, Stages of Job Loss)

In the late 1960s, Elisabeth Kübler-Ross published her seminal work, *On Death and Dying* (1969). On the basis of her series of interviews with terminally ill patients, Kübler-Ross theorized that dying patients progress through a series of five stages she termed *the stages of grief*:

1. Denial
2. Rage and anger

3. Bargaining
4. Depression
5. Acceptance (p. 100)

Although, fortunately, job rejection isn't as heartbreaking or as permanent as the death of a loved one, it can precipitate a serious depression. Our experience has been that many who have experienced rejection or termination in their careers have also experienced a grief similar to what Kübler-Ross described in her research. In reality, the stages of grief may arrive in phases, the griever may vacillate between stages, and grief may or may not proceed in sequential fashion. Still, the stages of grief can provide some insight in the aftermath of a job rejection. (*Note:* As we said earlier, these stages can easily be applied to job loss. If you have been downsized or fired, examine your own reaction to these stages.) For example,

- *Denial.* You hang up the phone or click out of your e-mail shocked that you weren't offered the job. Perhaps you briefly replay the rejection message, editing out the reality and replacing it with a job offer. This type of confabulating is common, in our experience. Or you convince yourself that you imagined the entire conversation. It couldn't really have happened the way you remember it.
- *Rage and anger.* "How could they offer the job to someone else?! Those #...! idiots!" Does this sound familiar? If you haven't given voice to these sentiments, you may have thought them. This stage is very brief for most. (Fortunately!) For others, even months after the rejection occurs, feelings of anger may well up without warning, and it might take awhile to connect the anger to the rejection.
- *Bargaining.* "I'll change." Reality has still not set in. We have counseled rejected applicants who continue to hold out hope even months later that the search committee chair will call to tell them the committee made a mistake and would like to offer them the job. Fortunately, most applicants work through this and other grief stages pretty quickly. In a few instances, however, we have witnessed rejected applicants enter a profound depression when the desired job didn't materialize.
- *Depression.* With rejected applicants, depression or sadness has usually been our sign that the applicant is moving through the stages of grief. Movement is the critical component to transitioning through disappointment. Shannon recalls a presentation by two monks—a Trappist and a Buddhist—who jointly expressed the maxim that "the only way out of pain and disappointment is through the crucible of pain and disappointment." In other words, people must embrace their hurts and disappointments to transcend them. In a sense, depression, in brief periods anyway, is likely a "good" sign, provided it doesn't last too long or become too severe.
- *Acceptance.* This stage is the end of the dark tunnel. Acceptance doesn't mean the absence of disappointment, pain, or bitterness. Rather, acceptance implies that the rejection no longer dominates your waking thoughts. After you have arrived at this stage on your journey through

disappointment, you have likely gained a healthier perspective on the process. This is the point at which you may begin to apply the lessons learned from the job rejection.

Most applicants for counseling positions will apply for a number of positions, most of which will net no job offers. That's why we recommend that your focus be on putting yourself in the position of being in the running for a job versus a job offer itself. We say this because each job advertised will garner a number of applications, yet typically only one candidate can be hired. These numbers usually translate into applicants applying for various and sundry position openings, and, one hopes, getting phone interviews, in-person interviews, and finally, an offer. Given that you had a phone interview and an on-site interview, you have done very well!

OK . . . so the hiring committee selected another candidate for the job you coveted and you feel demoralized. We understand that you are disappointed. What we plan on doing in this chapter is assist you in working through the disappointment of rejection, transforming that disappointment into positive action, and preparing for your eventual success in your continuing job search.

Why Job Candidates Are Rejected

There are a number of reasons for and variables in candidate rejection:

- *A more qualified candidate was selected.* Or the search committee *thought* another candidate was more qualified. Remember, picking the best candidate is an inexact science at best. What criteria constitute the "best candidate" are also debatable because hiring recommendations are made by search committees, composed of people who often have their own agendas and projections. Then you have the administrator who makes the final decision—and who may have a different view than the search committee.
- *One candidate was a better fit for the position.* This could be different than the preceding reason. Perhaps a candidate with fewer total years experience gets the offer because she has a counseling specialty area other candidates lack (e.g., trauma counseling, mediation experience, certification in play therapy) or, quite simply, she seemed to connect better with the committee or interviewer.
- *Fit has culture and gender implications.* For example, if all the counselors at the Best and Brightest Middle School are female (or vice versa), a male finalist probably has a better chance of being hired. The same maxim will often apply regarding culture and ethnicity. Now, it's likely that nobody will admit giving preference to candidates on the basis of gender, ethnicity, culture, and so forth, given legal and ethical considerations. But privately, search committees will take such gender, ethnicity, and cultural matters into consideration when making a hiring decision.
- *You were rejected because of racism, sexism, homophobia, and the like.* Although many schools, colleges, and treatment centers will welcome

cultural diversity, it's fair to say some won't, or that they will not accept *all* types of diversity. Although the counseling profession is generally a progressive one, not all counselors are affirmative in their action. Naturally, in many cases, administrators, and not counselors, will make the hiring decision.

- *The chosen candidate was simply better prepared than the others.* Bolles (2004) maintained that interview preparation is even more important than the candidate's qualifications. Incidentally, Shannon sat in on a recent interview where the most qualified applicant actually stated he "had not prepared much for the interview and would let his years experience speak for him." (The search committee did not look favorably on his lack of preparation.) Consequently, examine our sample interview questions in the text and practice in a mock interview setting at the career center or with friends or classmates. Remember, there is a reason athletes, musicians, and actors all practice before they perform. (*Note:* At times, I [Shannon] have had professors, colleagues, and students take issue with my referring to interviewing as a "performance," perhaps seeing the term as synonymous with *insincerity.* I would say, be yourself, but be your best self! Accentuate your strengths, and don't go into detail about your shortcomings. I see this as smart practice to follow.)

- *A candidate (or candidates) had a conflict with someone (e.g., search committee or director) during the interview.* The number one reason otherwise qualified professionals leave their job is because of conflicts with coworkers. Selection committees will carefully screen candidates for possible personality conflicts. So, be authentic and state your honest opinion, but work to come across as flexible and open with those expressing different views.

- *A candidate displayed inappropriate behavior during the interview.* Inappropriate behavior could include heavy drinking and making racist or sexist and other inappropriate comments. (*Note:* A few years ago, one very qualified finalist at Shannon's institution was dropped from consideration because he continually referred to women he'd dated and those he'd like to date. There's nothing wrong with dating, per se, but it is best not to mention it at an interview because your motives will likely be misunderstood.)

- *A candidate showed a lack of confidence at the interview.* You might be the most qualified candidate, but if you don't present as such, someone else will get the offer. If you consistently make self-deprecating comments during the interview process, it's likely this will be taken as lack of confidence. So, work to expunge self-critical comments (e.g., "It's nothing," "Anyone could have done it," "Oh, my colleagues really did most of the work"). Have a colleague, friend, or career counselor do a mock interview and critique you in this area. Don't be boastful, but do sound confident because you will be counseling students, families, groups, and couples, and they need to feel that you know what you are doing.

- *A candidate displayed discourteous behavior at the interview.* Such behavior includes being rude to the secretary or waiter, badmouthing past employers, or arguing with someone during the interview process. A good general interview guideline is to refrain from saying anything negative. Along the same lines, use good table etiquette when the search committee takes you to lunch or dinner. People skills are critical because no one really wants to work with a rude, obnoxious colleague.

- *A candidate was dishonest.* Were you caught in a lie regarding your résumé or curriculum vitae (CV)? Did you overly embellish your credentials during the interview process? Remember, the counseling world is still relatively small, and unethical interviewing behavior will almost always hurt you. Here's an example: A colleague of Shannon's received a call from a department chair at another institution. The chair informed his colleague that a finalist for an assistant professor position claimed to have cofounded a recent graduate program at his institution. The search committee chair was skeptical, however, and wanted to verify the applicant's claim. Shannon's colleague informed the chair that this claim was false. The applicant's ascending candidacy balloon abruptly burst.

- *A candidate's appearance was unprofessional.* Granted, attire for the counseling field is not the same as that for employees at Fortune 500 companies, but we recommend you play it safe at an interview. Men should wear a jacket, dress shirt, and tie, and women should wear a pants suit or skirt and jacket. Don't go overboard on cologne, perfume, or jewelry. After you're hired, you will have more freedom to express yourself in your dress. Another consideration is to examine how professionals dress at that particular school, agency, or counselor education department. If distance makes this impossible, then query a counseling professional holding a similar job for advice on interviewing dress.

- *The search was a failed one.* Sometimes a committee will not recommend a hire because of an unusually small pool of candidates or a general dissatisfaction with the finalists. In our experience, this happens most often in counselor education faculty searches or in P–12 school executive searches.

- *There was behind-the-scenes politicking.* You can never know the off-stage politics. Search committees are human, and they make mistakes. At times, someone above the search committee makes a mistake and hires a lesser recommended candidate. We have seen instances in which an executive, school superintendent, or dean hired a friend or family member. (Nepotism remains alive and well despite serious attempts to root it out!)

- *The candidate posted crude, lewd, or insulting information on Internet sites such as MySpace or Facebook.* Social networking sites have created blogs where anyone can post information or photos and hold online conversations. Some search committees are now conducting Google searches to root out potentially crude or embarrassing information regarding job applicants. If you use MySpace or another site, be discreet and anonymous or, better yet, don't post anything that might jeopardize your career.

Again, don't beat yourself up after a job rejection. You may well have done everything right. Perhaps you wrote a flawless résumé or CV, wrote an engaging application letter, interviewed splendidly, conducted yourself with impeccable behavior, and followed up the interview with a courteous thank-you note. Then, you eagerly anticipated the phone call that never came—until it was a rejection call. Perhaps the most painful words for a job candidate to hear may well be "and we're sorry to inform you we have offered the position to another candidate and she/he has accepted the job." On hearing these fateful words, your stomach may move north into your throat, your heart may pound, and your spirits may go into free fall. You may not even hear the caller's "and we wish you the best in future searches" spiel.

Remember, job rejection is a natural occurrence. Rejection is going to happen to you just as it has happened to us and to everyone who has ever applied for a job or promotion. Some job rejection is less painful than others. If you weren't terribly interested in the position but applied for practice, or lack of a better option, then maybe losing out isn't too bitter a pill to swallow.

It also depends on the stage of the application process. Getting weeded out before the interviewing process, although inherently disappointing, is likely easier to accept than being rejected after having interviewed. Typically, the closer you are to a job offer, the more painful the rejection. Naturally, we cannot promise to prevent feelings of disappointment or even depression if you are rejected for a job. When rejected for a job you want, you will feel sad—at least for a while. But the sadness will abate over time, especially if you continue to challenge yourself to apply for other job openings and actively work through some of the exercises in this text (or exercises in other texts that get you active). We can state with confidence, however, that we have some suggestions that can assist you in transitioning through the disappointment phase.

Career expert Tom Jackson (1981) has aptly characterized rejection in the job hunt by posing the question "Will you hire me?":

NO NO NO NO NO NO NO NO NO NO NO NO NO NO NO NO NO NO
NO NO NO NO NO NO NO NO NO NO NO NO NO NO NO NO NO NO
NO NO NO NO NO NO NO NO NO NO NO NO NO NO NO NO NO
NO NO NO NO NO NO NO NO NO NO NO NO NO NO NO NO YES!
(as cited in Bolles, 2004, p. 11)

Fortunately, you are very unlikely to be rejected at this many interviews—although some people have. (I [Shannon] have had plenty of job rejections myself and should I go on the job market sometime in the future, I would likely garner a few more.) We recommend you coach yourself to understand that a job rejection is simply one more "no" before an employer's "yes." Regardless of how long it takes you to land a job offer, it is important that you engage in self-care throughout the process.

Reframing

Counselors are part of a profession that practices the art of reframing, for example, when the rejected job applicant can restate his or her disappointment as something adaptive (Ellis, 1994). Reframing involves becoming mindful regarding one's own self-talk. People who are depressed and suffer from low self-esteem often engage in unrealistic, overly negative self-talk that focuses on their own failures and shortcomings (Ellis, 1994). Here, we provide an example of unrealistic, negative self-talk and how to reframe it into something healthier and more constructive:

> *Self-loathing response to job rejection.* I feel like a terrible failure because I failed to get the job I wanted.
> *Adaptive reframing response to job rejection.* It's unfortunate I did not receive the job I wanted. Although I'm disappointed, I will eventually find another job and the disappointment will lessen.

Albert Ellis also knew a lot about rejection. He was once quoted as saying he asked nearly 100 young women out before he landed his first date (He may have wanted to amend his approach!). Granted, interviewing is somewhat distinct from dating, but as with dating, you have to be vulnerable and risk disappointment if you are going to succeed. Dr. Ellis's personal narrative also makes a strong statement about the importance of resilience in the face of ongoing rejection.

Reframing is nothing new. It's been a part of the counseling–psychotherapeutic movement from the beginning and has its origins in the Greek philosopher Epictetus (Ellis, 1994). Restating Ellis (1994), people are not upset so much by the possibility of job rejection, but by their *perception* of job rejection. Once people explore the nature of job rejection, their depression and anxiety are likely to be reduced. In point of fact, every time Shannon has counseled applicants in the aftermath of a job rejection, he explores the client's *belief* about rejection because in his opinion it's the most important aspect of the counseling and debriefing process. Perhaps the most critical segment lies in the exploration of rejection and how people can transform their disappointment.

Transforming Disappointment: What Can You Do?

You have just received word that the school, agency, or college position you were banking on has been filled by another candidate for the job. You feel devastated and disoriented by the news. Dazed, you try to reconstruct what happened by replaying the interview over and over in your mind, trying to make sense of what went wrong. Once you work through the initial stage of the grief process, we recommend the following course of action.

- *Take some time to allow the shock to work through.* If you can, take a long walk or do something physical—something you ordinarily enjoy. Physical activity promotes relaxation and allows you to work off anxiety.
- *As soon as possible, process the news and disappointment with a close friend, partner, or spouse.* If you find it necessary, make an appointment with a counselor. Shannon has spent countless hours counseling disappointed job seekers. He has also spent a few sessions spilling out his own job rejection disappointment story!

- *When you have a little distance from the disappointment, reflect back on the interview.* What seemed to go well? What went less well? What could you improve on for next time?
- *Make a plan for self-care during this transitional time of disappointment (we illustrate a transitional plan later).* The critical emphasis here is to take an active role in transitioning from shock to acceptance. We recommend an in-depth process of self-reflection that creates support. We have created Exercises 5.1–5.5 for you to complete. (Use a separate sheet of paper if you need more room or copy this section.)

Exercise 5.1. Self-Assessment

How would you describe your current job or career situation?

_____

_____

_____

Ideally, where would you like to be in your professional life? Describe the job, possible location, salary, and anything else that seems pertinent.

_____

_____

_____

How can you begin to create the professional life you described above? In the space below, cite anything that will help you accomplish your professional goals.

_____

_____

_____

If you were recently rejected for a job (or jobs) you wanted, what did you learn that will help you in future job searches or interviews? Or, if you were recently fired, what did you learn that will assist you in achieving success in the next job?

_____

_____

_____

A staple of the solution-focused therapeutic movement includes scaling questions as a method of gauging current mood and progress in a counseling session (Walter & Peller, 1992). We recommend using Exercise 5.2 to gauge your present mood and optimism level. Then, as time passes, we recommend you revisit this exercise to gauge your improvement in mood.

Exercise 5.2. Gauging Mood and Optimism Level

1	2	3	4	5	6	7	8	9	10
Hopeless									*Very Optimistic*

In light of my recent job rejection(s), I feel _____ regarding my employment future.

Regarding the Kübler-Ross type of grief process described earlier, what stage are you currently in? Note the date of your answer to this question, then periodically return to assess whether your stage has changed and the reason for this change.

_____

_____

_____

What supports do you have for this employment transition? Examples of support can be family members, friends, spiritual community, co-workers, fellow grad students, an employment support group, or counselor.

_____

_____

_____

What personal strengths do you possess that will assist you in coping during this transitional period? Examples of personal strengths are a positive outlook, good work ethic, resiliency, coping skills, regular workout routine, or spiritual practice.

_____

_____

_____

How do you view this transitional period? Is it simply a bad experience? Does this period provide any avenues for professional and personal growth? Is there anything you look forward to during this interim period?

_____

_____

_____

Learning from past experience: Think about how you have coped with past transitions and disappointments. What's worked previously that might also be helpful in this situation? What new coping strategies might you use?

_____

_____

_____

Exercise 5.3. Reframing

It's human to engage in a period of self-criticism in the aftermath of a job rejection. What negative messages are you telling yourself (e.g., "I'm worthless!" "I'll never get hired!" "I won't be able to find another job!")?

_____

_____

_____

You want to reframe and transform negative messages into adaptive ones as we did earlier in the chapter. Use the space below to write the negative messages and their more adaptive reframe.

Note: Reframing will take regular practice before change is evidenced. (E.g., "It's unfortunate I did not get the job offer. Although I'm disappointed, what I learned from the process will assist me in my job search.")

_____

_____

_____

Naturally, transitional times are difficult. Can you talk with anyone who has successfully transitioned through his or her own job rejection or downsizing? If you are able to speak with someone, record below the most important tips you learned from that person's experience.

_____

_____

_____

Given the information gleaned from others, and the self-reflection exercises above, what could you work on to become a stronger job candidate and also to be a healthier, more resilient individual?

_____

_____

_____

The culture or meta-cultures we represent have a profound impact on our social, educational, spiritual, and vocational lives. Below list some cultural supports that assist you in your employment transition.

_____

_____

_____

During a transitional period such as a job search, it's very important to make time for yourself and those you care about. Achieving a sense of balance in your life is a noteworthy goal. What can you do to create a sense of balance in your life? (Or, if you feel you have been able to retain a balance among work, job search, school, and personal and spiritual life, how have you achieved that?)

_____

_____

_____

What else can I do to move through my frustration and disappointment?

_____

_____

_____

Exercise 5.4. Self-Reflection

Self-reflection is a critical skill, and every successful counselor, business person, executive, coach, and teacher engages in it.

Here we list several questions designed to assist you in both creating your career and helping you to examine your thoughts, opinions, ideas, and behavior and assess their congruence. We encourage you to spend some time answering the questions and also to consider sharing them with colleagues who might be struggling with their own job search.

- How can you start to create the career or job you desire (or "What's your career vision and how can you begin to achieve that vision?")?
- What talents and personal attributes do you possess that can assist you in creating your career vision?
- When you land this job, how will your life be different?
- When you have achieved your goal of becoming hired as a school, mental health, or rehabilitation counselor, how will you promote change among clients or students and the school, agency, or counseling center?
- When you picture the counseling profession in 10 years, what excites you? What challenges you? What changes do you need to make to be prepared?
- During this transitional time of a job search, what do you find most difficult? What is most rewarding about this time?
- Imagine potential employers responding positively to you. What would attract them to you?
- What resources can you tap into to create the counseling career you envision?
- Networking is an important component of a job search. What do you need to do to create an effective, supportive network (e.g., job search clubs, support groups, joining LinkedIn, etc.)?
- When conducting informational interviews, networking, or interviewing for a job, what message would you like to convey? How can you create that desired message?
- Think of times you achieved success. What worked? How can you improve and build on that success?
- When networking and interviewing, how optimistic do people find you? If you are unsure, how could you find out?
- What types of personal support do you need during this transition? How can you create the support you need?
- If you were looking to hire a counselor or counselor educator, what qualities would you be looking for? How well do you match up to these qualities? If you do not match up to some of the qualities you mentioned, what do you need to do to ensure you meet them?
- If an employer were to say, "Tell me five reasons why I should hire you?" how would you answer?

Another aspect of your job search to consider as you plan your "come-back" is your job search strategy. Although we wrote about strategy in an earlier chapter, this chapter seemed a more opportune location to discuss tinkering with your search. Heather Becker (1980/1999) developed the Assertive Job Hunting Survey (AJHS) to provide information about the manner in which people search for jobs. With Dr. Becker's permission, we have reprinted the survey here. We suggest you take the survey to get a sense of how assertive and active your search is.

Exercise 5.5. The Assertive Job Hunting Survey[1]

The AJHS was designed to by Becker (1980/1999) to provide information about the way in which you job search. Imagine yourself in each of these job hunting situations and indicate how likely it is you would respond in the described manner. As counselors, some of the items below will be more informative than others, as the AJHS provides a continuum for self-examination regarding job search assertiveness. If you have never job hunted before, answer according to how you would like to try to find a job. Please respond to the following statements by using the key below. The scoring key is placed at the conclusion of the survey.

1	2	3	4	5	6
Very Unlikely	Unlikely	Somewhat Unlikley	Somewhat Likely	Likely	Very Likley

_____ 1. When asked to indicate my experiences for a position, I would mention only my paid work experience.

_____ 2. If I heard someone talking about an interesting job opening, I'd be reluctant to ask for more information unless I knew the person.

_____ 3. I would ask an employer who did not have an opening if she/he knew of other employers who might have job openings.

_____ 4. I downplay my qualifications so that an employer won't think I'm more qualified than I am.

_____ 5. I would use an employment agency to find a job rather than apply to employers directly.

_____ 6. Before an interview, I would contact an employee of the organization to learn more about that organization.

_____ 7. I hesitate to ask questions when I'm being interviewed for a job.

_____ 8. I avoid contacting potential employers by phone or in person because I feel they are too busy to talk with me.

_____ 9. If an interviewer were very late for my interview, I would leave or arrange for another appointment.

_____ 10. I believe an experienced employment counselor would have a better idea of what jobs I should apply for than I would have.

_____ 11. If a secretary told me that a potential employer was too busy to see me, I would stop trying to contact that employer.

_____ 12. Getting the job I want is largely a matter of luck.

---

[1]Developed from "The Assertive Job Hunting Survey" by H. A. Becker, in _Career Tests: 25 Revealing Self-Tests to Help You Find and Succeed at the Perfect Career_ (pp. 113–117), by L. Janda, 1992, Avon, MA: Adams Media. Reprinted from _Measurement and Evaluation Guidance, 13_, 43–48, by H. A. Becker, 1980. Copyright 1980 by H. A. Becker. Reprinted with permission.

_____ 13. I'd directly contact the person for whom I would be working, rather than the personnel department of an organization.

_____ 14. I am reluctant to ask professors or supervisors to write letters of recommendation for me.

_____ 15. I would not apply for a job unless I had all the qualifications listed on the published job description.

_____ 16. I would ask an employer for a second interview if I felt the first one went poorly.

_____ 17. I am reluctant to contact an organization about employment unless I know there is a job opening.

_____ 18. If I didn't get a job, I would call the employer and ask how I could improve my chances for a similar position.

_____ 19. I feel uncomfortable asking friends for job leads.

_____ 20. With the job market as tight as it is, I had better take whatever job I can get.

_____ 21. If the personnel office refused to refer me to an interview, I would directly contact the person I wanted to work for if I felt qualified for the position.

_____ 22. I would rather interview with recruiters who come to the college campus or job fairs than contact employers directly.

_____ 23. If an interviewer says, "I'll contact you if there are any openings," I figure there's nothing else I can do.

_____ 24. I'd check out available job openings before deciding what kind of job I'd like to have.

_____ 25. I am reluctant to contact someone I don't know for information about career fields in which I am interested.

Scoring

Add your points for the following items: 3, 6, 9, 13, 16, 18, & 21. The remaining items (i.e., Items 1, 2, 4, 5, 7, 8, 10, 11, 12, 14, 15, 17, 19, 20, 22, 23, 24, & 25) are reverse scored. To obtain your points for these reverse scored items, subtract the number you indicated from 7. Add the subsequent numbers together and find your total score by adding the totals for the two clusters of items.

Norms

Score	Percentile
90	15
98	30
106	50
116	70
124	85

Summary of Scores

High scores indicate greater job hunting assertiveness. If, for example, you received a percentile score of 70, it means that 70% of people are *lower in job hunting assertiveness than you are*. For more information, see Becker (1980/1999).

In this book, we have tried to create a systematic profile for job search success. Use the AJHS to assess and revise your job search strategy. As we have also previously stated, get outside feedback from a career counselor, graduate school friend, professor, or older colleague in the profession regarding your job search strategy.

Allies and Role Models for Inspiration

Martha Lasley (2004) talked about the importance of selecting allies as a means of inspiration. Lasley encourages the people she coaches and advises to create such an inspiration list whenever they are contemplating change. Here, Shannon lists some of his allies and role models. Some of them are famous, and others are virtually unknown other than to him. All of those listed are individuals who displayed great courage, perseverance, and resilience in the face of serious obstacles.

- my grandparents, for raising five grandsons (one of whom was me);
- Rosa Parks, an ordinary woman who stood up for herself by sitting down and helped transform an entire society;
- Tich Nat Hahn, a Buddhist monk who has devoted a lifetime to cultivating peace;
- Mother Teresa, for rolling up her sleeves, fighting an impossible fight, and never surrendering to her doubts regarding faith, hope, and whether she could actually make a difference;
- Viktor Frankl, for his belief in personal meaning despite experiencing horrific trauma during the Holocaust;
- Martin Luther King Jr., for leading a peaceful revolution that hate could not snuff out;
- Shoshanna Cogan, my spouse, who is the embodiment of personal growth;
- Reese House, a former professor, who found time to care;
- the transit worker who collects tolls at the Grand Island toll booths who, despite a job involving mind-numbing sameness and dealing with the occasional verbal abuse, always brightened my day with her smile, warmth, and inner glow;
- Michael Casey, a fellow doctoral student at Oregon State University. At a coffee shop in Corvallis, Oregon, one summer, a group of skinheads were refused service. As management and others lined up to throw this group out, Michael, an African American with likely every reason to hate this group, asked whether he could buy them a cup of coffee. He spent almost 2 hours in dialogue with them, who were shocked that this object of their hatred reached out to them in kindness. "I just wanted to know why they hate me," he said. Michael's action may not have changed these skinheads, but it did establish the importance of dialogue and planted seeds of possibility in the group. (In fact, one of the skinheads admitted he would have to rethink some of his views.) Shannon calls dialoguing with adversaries the "Dr. Casey approach."

For me (Shannon), gathering my allies around me during transitional times provides inspiration and helps me tap into their courage when success is elusive and life seems unnecessarily unfair. Sometimes I might ask, "What would my grandfather do?" or "How might Viktor Frankl/Rosa Parks/Reese House handle this situation? Naturally, I don't really know what these people would do, but do I find calling on them emotionally and spiritually empowering. I suggest you identify personal and professional role models—they will not be perfect people because they are human. But good role models are out there, and using their examples, wisdom, and advice can be very comforting during difficult times.

Final Thoughts on Managing Difficulty

As a counselor, a large part of your job in any setting will be to assist students, clients, inmates, couples, groups, and so forth in moving through their own grief, pain, and disappointment. Fortunately, you get to move through your own personal phases of disappointment. Whenever you're tempted to give into resignation—or when one of your students or clients is—consider the following: Stay optimistic! Hope may very well be the best single predictor of success in any endeavor (Seligman, 1998). Thoroughly examine what you need to change to be more successful (as indicated by the preceding exercises), but also remember your existing strengths and work to build on them.

- *Remember, disappointment is transitory.* As with Kübler-Ross's (1969) stages of grief, everything will pass—perhaps not as quickly as you would like, but it will pass. Furthermore, you will have other opportunities for a new job, promotion, and so forth. Learn from your disappointment and be in a stronger position at the next opportunity.
- *Update your skills.* Are there trainings and certifications that might give you an edge in a competitive job market? Are you a certified mediator? Do you have training in play therapy or dialectical behavior therapy or another type of therapy? Have you been trained in addictions assessment? How much career or vocational experience and training do you have? Also, seek out the advice of someone in the field. Ask a veteran school, mental health counselor, counselor educator, or a counseling professional in your specialty what additional training or skills would make you a more competitive candidate. Learning and expanding your counseling career is a lifelong process both to obtain licensure and certification and to ensure you remain "alive" in your career.
- *Strategize.* Generate options for success and how to improve your chances of employment. This might mean revising your résumé or CV, practicing interviewing, practicing being at an interview dinner, or taking additional training. This time is when colleagues in the field are helpful. Also, solicit input from counselors who have landed jobs or senior colleagues who have a lot of experience in conducting interviewing and search committees.
- *Work on self-image.* Don't give in to negative self-talk. Shift your self-talk to indicate a more realistic, optimistic inner view. Remember, Ellis

(1994) has illustrated that unhealthy behavior often follows negative or unhealthy self-talk.

- *Practice, practice, practice.* Make use of role plays. For example, ask yourself what counsel you might give a friend of yours who was feeling as resigned as you feel presently, or remember Perls's (1969) classic Gestalt Empty Chair Technique and set up two chairs. In one chair, play the applicant, and in the other, play the interviewer. Play the interviewer giving feedback, and note your strengths, weaknesses, why they hired someone else, and so forth. You can give feedback to the interviewer from the perspective of what it's like to be the applicant and then ask questions, offer feedback, and so forth.
- *Remember your assets.* Don't dwell exclusively on deficits. Remember, to have gotten this far in your professional and educational life, you have to have had a lot of successes. Recount or list your successes. (Amy here: When I lost a major client, I sat down to brainstorm a list of all of my options, and I posted it over my desk. On the days when I didn't think I could pull it together—and there were quite a few of them for a while—I referred to the list. It reminded me that I was ultimately in charge of my own career and that I did have choices.)
- *Get or remain physically active.* If you have a regular workout routine, such as jogging, swimming, cycling, or walking, keep it up. If you do not have a fitness routine, find one you can commit to for a minimum of 3 days per week. You do not need to become a serious triathlete, but moderate exercise is good for your mental and emotional health. There really is something to releasing endorphins into your system. (And it prevents you from eating your way to a 20-pound weight gain in a depressed state.)
- *Create and nurture meaningful activities in your life.* If you have a spiritual or religious practice or community that you find supportive and helpful, then maintain that activity or community. Support groups can be important as well and are typically listed in the newspaper or on your city's Web site. Professional career and personal counseling are also recommended because conducting a job search can be very stressful. (Yes, you may be a counselor, but you shouldn't try to heal yourself. Everyone can benefit from counseling at some point in their life . . . even counselors!)

The most difficult days often yield the most growth. You have seen this with clients, and you can probably recognize it in your own personal experiences. As we look back on our own careers, we have learned the most during our most trying times. When Amy works with outplacement clients, she often tells them, "Six months from now, you'll be in a better place, and you'll look back at this day as the starting point of the life you want to live." As we leave this chapter, we leave you with this thought: When a door closes, don't sit in the darkness. Look for windows. That's where the light is shining through. You can examine things better in the light and see the opportunity just down the road.

Chapter

6

I'm Changing My Focus:
What Do I Do?

Plan B. The term is so commonly used in our lexicon, we rarely have to explain it. Plan B is what you use when Plan A isn't working anymore, for whatever reason. People change their focus as they develop new interests, as technologies are adapted for new uses, and as the economy—both macro and micro—changes. In this chapter, we consider how to effect a change in career focus.

More than 20 years ago in a graduate school class, I (Shannon) was listening to a talk given by the director of a local human services agency. The guest speaker, himself a graduate of the counseling program I was enrolled in, asked for a show of hands from the class regarding which of us planned on being a counselor? Virtually everyone, save a couple of student affairs majors, raised their hands, although most were somewhat puzzled at the seemingly obvious question.

"Okay," he continued, "Now, how many of you are planning on being administrators?" Less than a handful of the class lifted their hand. "All right; 5 years after graduation, two-thirds of you will be administrators like me," he replied.

A murmur of disbelief swept through the small, close-knit classroom. How could this man, a graduate of our counseling program, make such an egregious statement? Wasn't he supposed to be here to entertain us with uplifting alumni success stories and emphasize what a great choice we had made to enter the noble profession of counseling?

The speaker, realizing he had unleashed potential havoc in the room, then calmed us down and began to explain his prediction. He further clarified that as we gained several years experience, achieved licensure, and moved up in seniority, many of us would naturally move up in our respective agencies and schools. His point was that moving into administration was a natural progression for many counselors.

My (Shannon's) own experience has been that the guest speaker was spot-on in his prediction. My own career has witnessed my transition from student affairs administrator to community mental health counselor, director of a county mental health clinic, director of a university counseling center, and finally counselor educator—or at some times, performing in a variety of these different capacities simultaneously. I have also found many colleagues in the counseling field who have traveled a similar, though perhaps somewhat different journey on the road to career fulfillment.

Many professionals study or work for years in a particular career, then decide to change their career path or focus. In our experience, counselors are no exception to this rule. In our various and sundry wanderings inside and beyond the counseling profession, we have met numerous people who have changed careers multiple times. Sometimes the change is not greatly different: For example, Shannon has a colleague who earned a master's degree in school counseling and counseled in a school for a few years before switching to running a community-based mediation program. She continued to use many of the skills learned in her graduate program and honed in the field, although her job responsibilities and the people she served changed considerably. Many of you reading this text could cite your own stories of friends and relatives who have either changed careers or at least changed the focus of their career. Recently, Shannon met a colleague who had spent many years as an addictions counselor before returning to graduate school to become a school counselor because he decided he could be of more assistance counseling in a high school.

Transition in the counseling profession is certainly not new. Traditionally, teaching was the original path to school counseling, although that is no longer the only vehicle to becoming a school counselor. Counselors have moved into school and human services administration and become student affairs professionals or human resources directors, and the list goes on.

Therefore, it is likely, if not imperative, that you will change careers during your professional life. Some research has suggested that most people will have, on average, three to five careers (Bolles, 2004).

In 1978, Richard Nelson Bolles, author of the famed book *What Color Is Your Parachute?* published a popular text titled *The Three Boxes of Life and How to Get Out of Them.* The "three boxes" consisted of the educational box, from ages 0 to 18 (or 0 to 22 for college-bound students); the career box, from age 18 or 22 to 65; and the retirement box, from ages 62 to 65 or older. The career box was by far the largest because that box contained the most years of people's lives.

In the late 1970s, Bolles's book would have been accurate. In the 30 years since its publication, however, the career world has evolved drastically (Bolles, 2004). No longer do the majority of people work 35 to 40 years with one employer for the gold retirement watch. They are now likely to work for several employers, make multiple moves (including working overseas), change careers, and pursue more education than previous generations (Bolles, 2004).

Regarding education, nontraditional learners (those age 25 and older) have now become the majority population on college campuses (Pascarella & Terenzini, 2005). If Bolles were to rewrite *The Three Boxes of Life,* he might well title it *The Six to Eight Boxes of Life.*

Counselors, or those with a master's degree in counseling, planning a transition to a related field will need to bend their résumé or curriculum vitae (CV) to address the requirements of the job they seek. Here, we list some related jobs and fields counselors often go into:

- Student affairs professional (residence life, dean of students, student activities, college counselor)
- Community mediation (line mediator or director)
- Case manager or human resources worker or director
- Program director, assistant director, or director of a human services agency
- Corrections counselor or administrator (we list corrections counselor here because these positions are listed separately from other counseling positions)
- Adventure-based therapy (*Note:* Although we certainly consider this a therapeutic field, it has evolved separately from counseling)
- Athletic coaching
- Personal coaching
- Trainer or facilitator for for-profit and nonprofit organizations
- Community college instructor

It's also worth mentioning that many counselors transition from one field of counseling to another, for example, from

- school counselor to mental health counselor;
- mental health counselor to school counselor;
- school or mental heath counselor to college or community college counselor;
- college counselor to academic services counselor; and
- school counselor to employment counselor (often working in federally funded positions with displaced workers).

Preparing for the Transition

To prepare for a transition from counseling to a related, noncounseling field such as case management in a human services agency or student affairs administrator, you need to carefully examine the differences in responsibilities.

For example, if you worked as a case manager before you pursued graduate study in counseling, landing another position in case management probably won't be too difficult. In fact, a distinct percentage of Shannon's students are case managers and plan to remain so or plan to move up the ladder into management and run human services agencies. The master's degree in counseling often provides the necessary upward mobility for a trajectory into management in the schools and agencies.

Likewise, a number of Shannon's students have backgrounds in student affairs and plan to continue in roles such as dean of students and campus ombudsman in residence life. Again, a background in a related field plus a master's degree in counseling is usually very helpful because counseling is often recognized as a field that provides its students with broad training in human relations.

What is critical for the counseling graduate seeking a related career is an ability to articulate on a résumé and in an interview how his or her counseling skills are an asset for the position being sought. Consider this example:

> You have recently graduated from a counseling program with a master's degree, but you realized midway through your program you were not actually interested in a career providing counseling. You discover your real passion lies in working in the residence halls, using your communication skills mediating roommate conflicts, being an ear for students having personal or academic struggles, providing career advising, and being a referral resource for the university counseling center. During your last semester in grad school, while perusing the *Chronicle of Higher Education,* you notice a job advertisement that seems ideally suited for your interests, education, and background:

>> *Student Affairs:* Utopia Midwestern College in Idyllic, Iowa, is seeking an Assistant Director for the Department of Residence Life. Responsibilities include supervising Residence Directors (RDs) and Resident Assistants (RAs), oversight of judicial hearings, educational and health programming, RA/RD training, and other duties as assigned by the director. Qualifications include a master's degree in college student services, counseling, or a related field. Send a résumé/CV, letter of application, and three references to
>> I. M. Calm, Director
>> Utopia Midwestern College
>> Department of Residence Life
>> Idyllic, IA 66606
>> E-mail: jj@utopiamidwestern.edu

Naturally, your résumé or CV needs to reflect a fit for the position that has been advertised. Although communication skills are of critical importance in any student affairs position such as the one in this example, the primary duties would not be counseling, assessment, or diagnosing mental health issues. Your training and experience in counseling, however, could be a huge asset in a related field such as residence life.

Consider, for example, that roughly a third of college students meet criteria for a *Diagnostic and Statistical Manual of Mental Disorders* (4th ed., text revision)

Axis I mental health disorder (Kadison & DiGeronimo, 2004), and you potentially have a strong case. (*Note:* Identifying supporting information such as Kadison and DiGeronimo's book and select articles from the *Journal of College Counseling* also speaks strongly to broad reading in the field.) In the preceding example, a background in residence life is also crucial because counseling training alone will not be enough to make your candidacy serious.

Both Amy and I have backgrounds in student affairs, so we can speak with some degree of experience regarding this separate, though related, profession. If you are a student in a counseling program considering a career in student affairs, we recommend you get some tangible experience. Such experience could include a practicum or internship in the counseling or career services center or in one of the following departments: residence life, student activities, international education, or academic advising. Many counseling programs provide their students opportunities for additional training through advanced internships, individual studies, and other such options. Given the multifaceted careers most counselors will have in their working lives, our recommendation is that you seek out broad experiential training during graduate school.

You also need to be prepared for the reality that many vocational transitions will require additional education and training. Mental health counselors interested in school counseling will probably need an additional 1 to 1.5 years of education depending on the state in which they plan to work. The same could be said for school counselors interested in working in community mental health, especially given varying requirements for licensure.

Some related careers may not require additional education. Examples of this are some student affairs positions (e.g., academic advising), adventure therapy jobs, residential treatment positions (many of which require only a bachelor's degree), and addictions counseling.

The new field of personal coaching is currently very popular. Because personal coaching is quite similar to counseling, many counselors in private practice also provide coaching in addition to traditional counseling services. Thus far, however, few agencies, schools, and institutions are hiring personal coaches, with the exception of those working with people with developmental disabilities (these coaches are usually called job coaches, and their responsibilities are narrower than those of personal coaches). There appears to be no lack of private practitioners offering coaching services, if the advertisement sections of most newspapers and some magazines are any indication. If you plan to offer coaching services, be sure to check existing state laws. Although most states have established licensure standards for counseling, the field of coaching is largely unregulated. In accordance with the American Counseling Association's (ACA's; 2005) *Code of Ethics*, ensure before you offer a service that you have the training to offer it. We offer more on professional coaching later in this chapter.

What If I've Been Out of School for a Few Years? How Can I Get Into a Related Career?

In our experience, it is easier to get experience in related fields as a graduate student than as a postgraduate. When you are out in the marketplace and have a family, mortgage, and car payments, changing fields becomes more challenging, although it's not impossible.

Here's a case in point: Several years ago I (Shannon) received a call from a counselor wanting to transition into a career in a university counseling center. She was middle-aged and had no experience in college counseling. Her interest in college counseling had been stimulated through stories her husband, an academic administrator, would recount to her regarding student mental health issues. Somehow she heard of me and contacted me for career advice. We met, and I helped her to revise her résumé (which had not been updated in a good decade!) and to strategize how she could navigate the transition into college counseling. Because her spouse had a good salary, she was able to move from full-time to half-time work at her agency. Then she began soliciting informational interviews with area colleges and community colleges. With some 20 years of counseling experience, especially in treating serious mental health issues such as depression, anxiety, addictions, eating disorders, and sexual abuse, she was able to land a part-time position in a small college counseling center. Once she was in the door and her supervisor saw she was clinically skilled, she was able to increase her hours.

The chief difficulty in moving into some fields is that many counselors cannot afford an unpaid internship or survive on a part-time job with no health benefits. If you are young with no dependents, vocational mobility is far less complicated because you have no children to feed and no major impediment to a cross-country move. Still, many middle-aged adults are successful in transitioning to a different occupation. When contemplating a career change, we advise you carefully weigh the pros and cons of making such a career transition.

Considerations When Moving to a Related Career

There are several issues for counselors to consider before making a move to a different or related career:

- What are your chances of landing a job within 6–12 months?
- Where are the jobs advertised?
- What are the skills, experience, and requirements for the job or career?
- What professional organizations exist? Which should you join?
- What's the U.S. Department of Labor's occupational outlook for this field? (This is a critical aspect to check out.)
- Would this transition require more education? If so, how much? What is the approximate investment necessary to pursue this training? Would you be able to recoup this over a period of months? Years?
- Whom do you know who is currently employed in the field you are considering? We strongly suggest you speak with them regarding the field, issues, additional training, job availability, and so forth.
- Would you need to move for this career? How far? The next state or across the country?

- Have you completed an informational interview with someone in the field to gauge the pros and cons of the job?
- Have you retrofitted your résumé or CV and letter of application to match the requirements of the field?
- What type of low-cost training is available that would make you a more competitive candidate? What additional skill sets do you already possess that would be marketable in this field?
- Why would you want to make a career move? Better money? More stability? More available jobs? Something else? (If so, what?)

Joining a Professional Counseling Organization

Many of you may be considering a specific career move. In the next section, we provide more food for thought regarding career transitions.

In addition, because professional organizations are the lifeblood of a profession, we urge you to join the ACA and the professional affiliate division representing the counseling field you are interested in (e.g., the American Mental Health Counselors Association [AMHCA] for mental health counselors, National Career Development Association [NCDA] for career counselors and consultants, American College Counseling Association [ACCA] for college counselors). Professional organizations publish journals (e.g., *Journal of Counseling & Development, Journal of Mental Health Counseling*), hold annual conventions, maintain helpful Web sites, and lobby Congress and state legislatures to advocate for a stronger profession. One of the best actions you can take both for your career and your profession is to join ACA or (as of 2009) one of its 19 affiliate organizations.

Membership in a professional counseling organization such as ACA or the Association for Counselor Education and Supervision also makes the statement to potential employers that not only have you earned a graduate degree, but you are also connected to the profession of counseling, take and read research on cutting-edge issues in counseling, and are aware of emerging trends in the field. Membership in ACA or its affiliates does not prove you will be a better counselor, but it does make a statement regarding how seriously you take your profession. As professionals who have hired counselors, we can attest that membership in appropriately related professional associations is a positive attribute. Conversely, lack of membership in a professional organization is a detriment to your candidacy.

Specific Categories of Jobs

Research Positions in Counseling or a Related Field

Many, although not all, such research positions require a doctoral degree. Most research will be conducted in large research universities or governmental agencies such as the National Institute of Mental Health, National Institutes of Health, and others. Research positions are very competitive and may involve related skills such as strong statistical skills and grant-writing experience. Research positions will be most congruent for doctoral-level counselors who enjoy research but are unsure about teaching in a graduate program or working in the mental health field. We recommend you speak with your major professor regarding research positions, or, if you have been out of graduate school for a few years, contact the National Institute of Mental Health or another governmental agency regarding such positions. In our experience, research positions at major universities and with the federal governmental are very competitive.

International Counseling

The counseling profession has become a global industry. Counselors interested in working abroad should carefully consider geographic, cultural, social, language, religious, and other challenges. The International Association for Counselling (IAC) is a good organization to join should you be contemplating counseling work overseas. Also, if you are interested in relocating to a particular country or region, it would be prudent to join a counseling organization in that country or region and use that organization for networking. Be aware that counseling requirements vary considerably from one country to another, as do emigration requirements. Also, the international counseling market is still small, although it should improve in the next decade. Because of the relative newness of this field, salary ranges are difficult to define. If you know what country you may be emigrating to, you might do a key word search. For example, if you are interested in moving to Australia, search on "occupational outlook for counselors in Australia." Workforce Australia, the Australian equivalent of the U.S. Department of Labor's Bureau of Labor Statistics, may be able to provide some of the information you seek.

Living abroad also can be very stressful; you will be isolated from family, close friends, and familiar geography while you adapt to a different culture. Countries that have radically different cultures, laws, and social customs will also present additional challenges. For example, relocating from, say, Buffalo, New York, to Toronto, Canada, will naturally be an easier transition than that from Buffalo, New York, to Singapore. We recommend you carefully consider the pros and cons of such a move. Are you ready to start over and move to a faraway country with no relatives or close ties? Do you have the financing to move to a distant country? What assistance would you be receiving if you landed a job overseas? Professional counseling, or at the very least discussing the matter with a trusted colleague or someone who has worked overseas, would be a worthy course of action for anyone considering moving to another country.

School Counseling

Professional counselors considering a transition to school counseling will probably need additional education, including a practicum and internship in a school setting. Demand for school counselors varies considerably, with urban schools offering the majority of open positions. Some regions of the United States, most notably the South and the Sunbelt, will have more openings for school counselors than other regions of the country.

According to the U.S. Department of Labor (2008), school counseling is expected to grow only 13% over the next decade. Although this represents moderate, steady growth, it is significantly less optimistic than occupational projections for addictions counseling and mental health counseling.

School counselors work 9-, 10-, and 12-month contracts depending on the school or school district. With few exceptions, counselors in private schools will earn considerably less in salary than counselors in public schools, although they will have a more manageable student-to-counselor ratio. The median salary for school counselors is around $53,000, but salaries will vary considerably depending on the location, school district, public versus private school, urban versus suburban setting, and so forth.

Private schools are also a career option, and many counselors are employed in private P–12 schools. Many, if not most, private schools are sectarian in nature, and this might pose a challenge for counselors who do not share the school's religious beliefs and practices. Because sectarian schools do not receive public tax dollars, salaries are considerably lower than at their public counterparts.

Student enrollments are smaller at private schools, however, and many counselors may potentially find private schools more intrinsically rewarding because there may be more time for personal, academic, and career counseling. It is also fair to say that, because of the cost of private schools, students there are more likely to be from upwardly mobile families and possess higher academic and career expectations.

Private schools usually advertise in local newspapers, sectarian newspapers, and newsletters (e.g., those of Catholic, Jewish, or Muslim groups). In many cases, counselors working in sectarian schools are not required to share the religious faith of the particular school, although more conservative religious-based schools will likely require the counselor to be of their faith. Direct application is often a successful method for attaining employment with these types of institutions. Networking within this system (e.g., membership and activity at a church, temple, or mosque) can help, as can serving on appropriate boards in these types of institutions.

Although the *Occupational Outlook Handbook* (U.S. Department of Labor, 2008) did not list salary earnings for counseling positions in private P–12 schools, given that private schools typically pay employees less such positions may open with regularity because many private school counselors often transition to better paying public school positions.

Mental Health Counseling

Counselors moving from a different counseling specialty to mental health counseling will probably need additional coursework, particularly a practicum and internship in a mental health setting. Naturally, you would also want to check state licensure requirements, so getting a copy of ACA's (2008) *Licensure Requirements for Professional Counselors: A State-by-State Report* is a good idea.

The *Occupational Outlook Handbook* (U.S. Department of Labor, 2008) has projected mental health counseling to be one of the fastest growing mental health fields, with a growth rate projection of 30% over the next decade. Currently, mental health counselors are licensed in 49 states; Washington,

DC; Puerto Rico; and Guam (California remains the lone state with no counselor licensure). Mental health counselors number roughly 100,000 in the United States, although this number is likely to grow considerably over the next decade (U.S. Department of Labor, 2008). Mental health counselors may also discover that it is relatively easy to move into closely related fields such as addictions counseling.

The American Mental Health Counselors Association (AMHCA) is the primary professional organization for mental health counselors. AMHCA is also an ACA affiliate, although AMHCA collects it own dues and holds a separate convention in the summer. Jobs for mental health counselors certainly are available provided one is willing to relocate, take additional graduate course work, and in some cases take a temporary reduction in salary. (School counselors, e.g., will typically earn considerably more money than mental health counselors and will have summers off.) In our experience, beginning salaries can range from $25,000 to $45,000, depending on the region of the country and the type of agency. The U.S. Department of Labor puts the median salary for mental health counselors at $34,500. Mental health counselors who become licensed and garner several years experience may have the option to move into supervisory and administrative roles and consequently receive a higher salary.

Addictions Counseling

Counselors considering a move to the field of addictions should be aware that this is the fastest growing mental health field of all, with a projected growth rate of 34% over the next decade (U.S. Department of Labor, 2008). Because addictions counselors may hold a master's degree, bachelor's degree, associate's degree, or no degree, salaries generally are considerably less than for other types of counseling.

The U.S. Department of Labor (2008) reported the median salary for addictions counselors to be $30,000. For counselors who make a career in the addictions field; obtain a master's degree, licensure, and national certification (certified addictions dependency counselor); and move into management, earnings can increase significantly.

Naturally, because of the nature of addictions, co-occurring disorders, relapse rates, and initial lower pay, burnout rates for addictions counselors tend to be high. Previously, being in recovery from a chemical substance addiction (alcohol, methamphetamines, nicotine, etc.) was considered a requirement for entry into this field, although this is no longer a barrier for counselors interested in entering the addictions field. Addictions counselors have historically not been required to have a master's degree, although this seems to be changing in some regions of the country. It is also accurate to state that addictions counselors with a master's degree will have more potential for advancement because of credentialing (e.g., licensure). Master's-level counselors of all types are eligible to enter this field, and jobs are plentiful in almost all regions of the country (U.S. Department of Labor, 2008). Counselors with a master's degree in mental health counseling may have the easiest transition to the field because of the relative similarity in training and job settings.

The U.S. Department of Labor (2008) has estimated the number of addictions counselors at more than 80,000, and this number could significantly increase over the next decade. Because of emphasis on addictions treatment, counselor burnout, and the expanding nature of addictions, jobs are likely to be more plentiful in the addictions field than in any other counseling field. The International Association of Addictions and Offender Counselors (IAAOC) is the primary counseling organization for addictions counselors, although addictions counselors can hold memberships in the AMHCA, ACA, and various other addictions treatment organizations.

Rehabilitation Counseling

Rehabilitation counseling is a specialized field within counseling, usually requiring a master's degree or higher in rehabilitation counseling. Counselors transitioning from related fields would be required to take additional course work, including a separate practicum and internship.

In addition to licensure (e.g., licensed professional counselor, licensed mental health counselor), the national certification (certified rehabilitation counselor) is considered very important for rehabilitation counselors. Rehabilitation counselors work in both inpatient and outpatient settings and for public and private agencies, assisting disabled clients dealing with or adjusting to acute or chronic disorders. Some rehabilitation counselors have a particular focus, such as counseling people who are deaf or hard of hearing, people who are visually impaired, or people with mobility challenges.

The U.S. Department of Labor (2008) has estimated that some 141,000 rehabilitation counselors are employed in the United States, and growth rates are projected at 23% for the next decade. The median salary is approximately $30,000, although it is considerably higher for rehabilitation counselors with 5 or more years of experience. The American Rehabilitation Counseling Association (ARCA) is the flagship organization for the field of rehabilitation counseling. Naturally, we encourage you to join this organization if you are interested in rehabilitation counseling.

College and University and Community and Technical College Counseling

Counselors hoping to break into higher education will definitely find the job market challenging, although jobs in 2- and 4-year colleges are available provided aspiring college counselors are willing to move anywhere. There is also no doubt that the surest route to a career in college and university counseling lies in strategic, front-end planning on the part of the aspiring counselor.

Most college and university counselors likely spent their graduate practicum and internship in a college or university counseling setting (whether it be a 2- or 4-year institution). Our experience is that college counseling professionals prefer counselors with collegiate counseling backgrounds because counselors with a working knowledge of higher education are generally preferred over counselors from outside areas (e.g., school counselors, mental health counselors).

Counselors with previous work experience or graduate school experience in college counseling centers, residence life (resident assistant or resident director), dean of students office, or career center will have a distinct advantage over those lacking a background in one of these areas. A strong preference for hiring psychologists and doctoral-level clinicians (e.g., social workers and counselors with doctorates) to staff 4-year college counseling centers remains, although master's-level counselors have made significant inroads (Gallagher, 2007), particularly in colleges with enrollments of fewer than 5,000 full-time equivalents. For planning's sake, the master's degree, coupled with previous college counseling or student affairs experience, is the minimum requirement in this field, with a clear preference for doctoral-level psychologists (i.e., PhD, PsyD). For counseling centers at community and technical colleges, master's-level counselors, as opposed to psychologists and social workers, appear to be the clear majority. In 2-year colleges, counseling is more heavily focused on career and vocational issues than on personal ones. Naturally, this dynamic may change with time because mental health issues continue to be in the headlines.

The U.S. Department of Labor (2008) did not break down numbers of college and university counselors, although with some 4,000 colleges, universities, and 2-year community and technical colleges, we would estimate the field to have some 12,000 to 15,000 professionals. The U.S. Department of Labor put median earnings at $41,780 for 4-year institutions and roughly $48,240 for 2-year colleges. The American College Counseling Association (ACCA) is the primary professional organization for this field, although because of its relatively young age (it was founded in 1991) and because of tradition, the American Psychological Association (APA) carries more clout with college counseling professionals and student affairs administrators. As the counseling profession evolves, however, ACCA will likely become a more influential organization.

College counseling positions are highly competitive, although breaking into college counseling in later years might be accomplished through part-time or contractual work (especially in the area of addictions counseling, which is frequently subcontracted), returning for a graduate certificate, and doing an internship in a colleague setting.

Occupational outlook projections for college counseling were not available from the U.S. Department of Labor (2008), but counselors with the ability to relocate will have a much better chance of securing employment than those who are restricted to a particular geographic location. College counseling positions are usually advertised in the *Chronicle of Higher Education*'s weekly newspaper or through their online edition (www.thechronicle.com). Master's-level counselors will likely have more success in achieving employment in centers at colleges with enrollments of fewer than 5,000 students and if they are licensed, have previous counseling experience in a college setting (or have completed a practicum and internship in a college setting), and have some background in addictions and residence life.

We also recommend, as with all counseling areas, that you speak with a counseling professional working in college counseling for advice, tips, and information regarding how to break into this area.

Creative Arts Counseling and Therapy

Creative arts counselors represent a relatively new counseling profession. Creative arts counseling includes art therapy, music therapy, play therapy, dance therapy, and others. Some states now license creative arts counselors separately from mental health counselors, although many others allow counselors from various fields to practice provided they have training in the respective creative arts therapy field. (Check your respective state counselor licensure laws.)

Mental health counselors, school counselors, and others may be able to practice as play therapists or art therapists with nondegree certificate training. For example, the University of North Texas offers credentials in play therapy, as do many other traditional and online institutions. Some traditional counseling programs now include art therapy or play therapy degree lines or certification in their curriculum. In many cases, mental health counselors, rehabilitation counselors, school counselors, and such may integrate creative arts counseling into their work. For example, the elementary school setting would likely be a natural place to use art therapy or play therapy. Some hospitals may hire art therapists to work with psychiatric populations or with less verbal patients (e.g., those with autism spectrum disorders)

The U.S. Department of Labor (2008) did not list creative arts therapists separately from other counselors, so job projections and salary range may be difficult to gauge. For additional information, some notable professional organizations related to creative arts therapy are

- American Art Therapy Association (AATA; www.arttherapy.org/);
- American Dance Therapy Association (ADTA; www.adta.org/);
- American Music Therapy Association (AMTA; www.musictherapy.org);
- Association for Play Therapy (APT; www.a4pt.org); and
- Sandplay Therapists of America (STA; www.sandplay.org/).

College Student Personnel or Student Services Professional

Student personnel is a broad term covering professions ranging from academic advising to counseling center, career center, disability services, dean of students, residence life or residence education, and student activities. Outside of career and personal counseling centers, most student affairs professionals prefer to hire graduates with master's degrees in college student services, college student development, or adult education as opposed to professionals with counseling degrees. Alternate backgrounds for career development can also include student personnel administration, human resources, organizational development, and business administration.

Traditionally, many counselors have had a background in college student personnel (as did both of us), especially as resident advisors working in college student housing. There are still some master's-degree counseling programs with the title of counseling and college student services administration, although this is an exception in the contemporary era. Counselors with strong student affairs backgrounds obtained in undergraduate and graduate work, however, will have a very good chance of being hired into the field. It is also fair to state that given the high incidence of mental disorders among current college students (Kadison & DiGeronimo, 2004), any college administrator with a background in mental health would be at an advantage in the job market. The U.S. Department of Labor (2008) has estimated that student personnel services will grow at a slower rate than most counseling fields, with a projected growth rate of 14%. What is also unknown is how the move toward online education will affect student affairs professionals, although it is likely there will be some contraction in the next decade. That being said, even Web-based institutions do hire student affairs staff, especially those with experience in career counseling and academic advising. Some 131,000 student affairs professionals are employed in colleges (2 and 4 year) and universities in the United States.

Because of the variation in student affairs fields and levels of responsibility, salaries will vary considerably. Directors and assistant directors in student affairs earn very good salaries, although competition for such jobs is, in our experience, very high. Counselors interested in student affairs careers should join the American College and Personnel Association (ACPA), the National Association of Student Affairs Professionals (NASPA), or one of the national specialty area organizations (e.g., Association of College and University Housing Organizations International [ACUHO-I], Association of College Unions International [ACU-I]). College student services job vacancies are generally advertised in the *Chronicle of Higher Education* and at www.higheredjobs.com. The best advice regarding a job search for student affairs positions is to begin your search in the fall by regularly checking the *Chronicle of Higher Education*'s online edition (and www.higheredjobs.com). Vacancies are usually filled by late spring. Screening interviews often take place at national conferences such as those of the ACPA, NASPA, and ACU-I, so the ability to attend these events is advantageous.

Community Mediation

Mediation is becoming a popular field in the United States. Although data on numbers were unavailable, our personal experience is that this is a growing field. Most mediation jobs will likely be in community agencies, as opposed to colleges and P–12 schools.

Because graduate degree programs in mediation are rare, mediators come from a variety of fields: business, social work, psychology, criminal justice, student affairs, and, of course, counseling. Mediation is used in business and industry, higher education, federal government, community service organizations, divorce proceedings, and so forth.

Some counseling programs now require mediation training either as part of the curriculum or as a continuing education unit. Some states now require mediators to be state certified to receive court referrals or advertise themselves as mediators. Some counselors in private practice also offer mediation services along with individual, couple, family, and group counseling.

Mediation and counseling require many overlapping skills. Any couples or family counselor should be well versed in mediation. Counselors wishing to move into this separate area should seek to become state certified (if offered) and receive additional educational training and supervision in mediation. Most medium- to large-size cities will have public mediation centers where counselors can volunteer to gain oversight and experience.

There are also a number of professional mediation organizations. Some notable ones are

- Association for Conflict Resolution (ACR; www.acrnet.org);
- CPR International Institute for Conflict Prevention and Resolution (CPR; www.cpradr.org);
- National Association for Community Mediation (NACM; www.nafcm.org);
- Victim Offender Mediation Association (VOMA; www.voma.org); and
- Victim Offender Reconciliation Program (VORP; www.vorp.org).

No occupational outlook statistics were available from the U.S. Department of Labor (2008), although mediation has become a popular service in many communities. Mediation jobs will likely be advertised in local newspapers. Direct application to law practices that are known to handle a number of divorce or child custody cases may also be an effective means of identifying opportunities. Social services organizations sometimes hire mediators to work with divorcing couples, small claims courts, VORP, and the like. Community mediators are also likely to enter the mediation field through a separate profession such as law, counseling, social work, or corrections because few graduate programs in mediation exist at the collegiate level. Counselors interested in mediation should check with local mediators for advice on how to break into this profession. Generally, mediators must complete a training and certification process.

Jobs for mediators are most often advertised in local newspapers or their online edition. Counselors interested in applying for mediation jobs should also be a member of a professional mediation organization (such as those listed earlier), be certified, and have some actual documented experience in mediation.

Counseling in Correctional Facilities

Many well-paying jobs are available in jails, state and federal prisons, and inpatient residential treatment facilities. Our experience is that many counselors prefer working with nonmandated clients, although we would encourage counselors to consider the corrections population.

Inmate populations lack adequate job skills and struggle with addictions, depression, sexual offenses, anxiety, grief, separation from their families, and loss of freedom. Working in a correctional facility can certainly be challenging from a number of standpoints. If you are considering such a career move, talk with counselors who work in correctional settings. Some basic issues to be aware of are limits of confidentiality, administrative support, punitive versus therapeutic approaches, and the safety risks of counseling in correctional facilities, to name a few.

Although the U.S. Department of Labor (2008) did not compile separate pay statistics or employment figures for counselors in correctional settings, our experience has been that correctional settings generally offer competitive pay and a good benefits package. The principal professional organization for counselors in this field is the International Association of Addictions and Offender Counselors (IAAOC).

Counselors should be aware of the special environment and limitations in working with inmate populations. In most cases, confidentiality between the counselor and the client is very different from that in traditional settings. The primary client may actually be the prison or parole board, not the inmate or inmates before you. Although hard figures are difficult to come by, our experience has been that jobs are available for counselors desiring to work in correctional settings. It would be helpful to have worked in a prison or jail or to have completed a practicum or internship in a correctional facility. The lack of work experience in a corrections environment would not prevent a counselor from becoming employed in such a setting. Counseling positions are usually advertised in local newspapers, the employment office, through job training agencies, and the like. We also advise you to speak with a corrections counselor and get a sense of the issues, limitations, and risks of working in a prison. In some cases, prisons also contract with local mental health providers who provide counseling services.

Professional Coaching

Professional coaching has become a popular area of interest and practice in the United States. Coaches may come from disparate fields such as management, health care, recreation, and so forth; however, many are trained counselors. In many instances, professional counselors in private practice offer professional coaching as an ancillary service much in the way they offer mediation.

Although counseling has traditionally focused on empowering the client to move from a state of dysfunction to function in the areas of education, mental health, and career, coaching has a narrower focus and is likely more concerned with improvement in job performance or attaining personal goals. Professional coaches often work with clientele in identifying, setting, and strategizing how to achieve goals in their personal or professional life. The process of coaching may involve activities similar to counseling, such as active listening, problem clarification, homework, risk taking, and career or personal visioning, although coaching is not focused on mental health issues.

Because this is a new field, with multiple professionals involved in providing coaching services, counselors interested in coaching should first attempt to clarify their particular area of interest. The International Coach Federation (ICF) is perhaps the largest and best known professional and credentialing organization for personal coaches. ICF offers training, certification, a conference, and many other options. ICF has three levels of credentialing:

1. *Associate certified coach.* Requires 60 hours of coach-specific training and 100 hours of coaching experience with at least eight clients.
2. *Professional certified coach.* Requires 120 hours of coach-specific training and 750 hours of coaching experience with at least 25 clients.

3. *Master certified coach.* Requires 200 hours of coach-specific training and 2,500 hours of coaching experience with at least 35 clients (Ellis, 2008).

Note that all hours are *clock* hours, not *credit* hours.

The ICF also sets objectives for professional and ethical behavior. Counselors interested in coaching should contact the ICF for more information (www.coachfederation.org) and seek out professional coaches in their geographical area. Because coaching is a new occupation, the U.S. Department of Labor (2008) did not list any information on it. Counselors who provide coaching services should be careful to explain to potential employers how coaching differs from counseling.

What Revisions Should I Make to My Résumé or CV?

If you are changing counseling fields, or moving to one of the related careers we have discussed, overhauling your résumé or CV does not generally present a difficult challenge. If you have an electronic résumé or CV—which is common in today's job market—then your focus will primarily be simple revision.

First of all, review your résumé or CV both for accuracy and to see whether it presents you in the manner in which you intend. Then take a look at the examples provided in the text to ensure you have a viable résumé or CV format. If you are targeting a position as a mental health counselor when your previous career or position was in school counseling, then your résumé will require slight revisions. The biggest change may be the job objective section. Because community mental health and addictions counseling emphasize psychotherapy over traditional school counseling roles of career and academic counseling, you will need to tailor your résumé and cover letter accordingly.

If you are applying for a position in community mediation, you would be wise to market your skills, training, and experience in conflict resolution, facilitation, counseling, and the like. If you are applying for a position in student affairs, whether in the counseling center or elsewhere, emphasize your experience in and education for the particular position and also highlight your experience in higher education.

Essentially, whenever you apply for a job, it's up to you, the applicant, to demonstrate your fit for the advertised position, both in the cover letter and later in an interview. You should also be aware that there are few, if any, perfect "fits" for a job. In our own vast experience serving on search committees, most successful candidates will not match up to all desired qualifications. Having made this statement, however, we should mention that serious candidates will meet most qualifications for the advertised position. So, when you are undecided about whether to apply, our guideline is to go ahead if you meet, say, 60% of the qualifications. With today's electronic submissions, you're not even out the postage costs!

Do Counselors Actually Have Success Moving to Different Fields?

Absolutely! Both of us are proof that counselors can and often do switch fields and are successful in this process. Actual numbers are difficult to track, but in our experience in counselor education, human resources, community mental health, student affairs, and school counseling, many of our colleagues have switched counseling areas and fields with success. In many cases, it may take some time to land a job in a related profession or field.

Here's a commonsense tip: If you are considering moving from, say, school counseling to addictions counseling, have someone in the addictions field look over your résumé and cover letter. Then ask someone in the field for an informational interview.

Many agency managers will be willing to speak with you, and informational interviews are how you can glean valuable information from professionals in the field. Ask them what you would need to do to get hired in their profession. After all, the best resources are professionals currently in the field.

The good news for aspiring counselors is that counseling is an expanding field (U.S. Department of Labor, 2008). Counseling training and experience also provide a broad array of skills useful for many human services positions, such as case managers, student affairs professionals, mediators, and human resources directors. Your transferrable skills, when communicated appropriately through a cover letter, résumé or CV, and interview, will ultimately help you succeed in making your career transition.

Considerations
for Self-Employment

Once upon a time when I (Amy) was working as a career counselor on the campus of a private college in the Midwest, I decided to create my own dream job, as I often advised the many students who came through my office to do. First, I determined what I thought I did best and wanted to incorporate into my dream job:

- Help people to identify their strengths and teach them how to market themselves so they could earn a living
- Create new and different ways to teach individuals about career exploration
- Administer a series of projects that would provide me with the variety I crave
- Write!

In addition to these "what I *did* want" factors, there were a few things I was ready to give up:

- The bureaucracy and meritocracy I experienced on the administrative side of higher education
- Long daily drives to and from campus
- Repetitive academic schedules (my job was beginning to feel a little bit like that old Bill Murray movie, *Groundhog Day*)
- Pantyhose and high heels

In short, I wanted to continue doing what I was doing, but on my own terms, according to my own schedule, and in jeans, a sweater, and comfortable shoes. I don't know that I would have used the term *self-employment* to describe my dream job in those days, but the work that I do now encompasses all of the elements that I felt were important even then, and it allows me the flexibility in my schedule that I appreciate as a parent of school-age children.

I love what I do *and* how I do it. As a career consultant, I believe that everyone should feel the same way about *their* job, and if they don't, I believe they should find a different way to earn a living.

Still, self-employment, with all of its intrinsic rewards, also has its drawbacks. If I don't keep it in check, my workday could start before the sun rises and end as David Letterman is wrapping up his monologue. Between the two ends of the day, I juggle work, home, and volunteer projects and monitor four e-mail accounts, three phone lines, a fax machine, and the business news network. I have worn out two laptops, an auxiliary computer keyboard, and several cell phones in the past 5 years.

Recently, I laughed out loud when I heard someone quip, "I started my own business so I could work half-days whenever I wanted. Nobody told me that I would have trouble figuring out which 12 hours a day to work!"

This chapter addresses self-employment, and for most readers that may mean private practice. Others may be interested in exploring more nontraditional applications of their skills in various marketplaces. Because both Shannon and I have personal experience in self-employment, here we identify the risks and rewards, sharing some of our stories (the good, the bad, and the ugly, as they say), our observations, and our professional recommendations. Our focus is self-employment as a career choice. (If you are interested in step-by-step instructions on how to make a private practice work, our good friends Bob Walsh and Norm Dasenbrook are widely considered in the counseling profession as the foremost experts, and we heartily recommend the materials they have available, which are referenced in the Appendix.)

Launching a Career in Private Practice

Searching for a job in private practice is considerably different from looking for a position with a school or agency. In my (Shannon's) nearly 2 decades of teaching in higher education, I would estimate that about 70% of my students have mentioned opening a private practice as a professional goal. Most students, however, do not understand all the issues and complexities (legal, ethical, financial, etc.) involved in private practice. The reality is that many counselors are interested, although few can hang a shingle and make it a success.

Private practice is a very different type of market from any other counseling work because you are either planning a solo operation or contemplating going into practice with several colleagues. You probably won't run across notices to join a private practice in the classified ads section of the local paper, either. Private practice tends to be a closed market where entry requires that an established counselor demonstrate his or her marketability to an association of private practitioners or have the capital—professional *and* financial—to open his or her own private practice. Networking skills are paramount if joining an established practice is your goal.

Many counselors have branched out from careers in counselor education, school counseling, mental health, and college counseling into private practice. Private practitioners tend, by necessity, to be experienced clinicians. Counselors coming straight from a master's degree program are usually not ready for private practice because they have neither the practical experience nor the experience required for licensure as a professional counselor. In most states, counselors must be licensed to operate a private practice.

Anecdotally, we have observed that many counselors operate a small counseling or consulting business as ancillary income, with salaried jobs in a school, agency, or college as their main source of revenue. These counselors are wading into private practice as opposed to diving into it. In every location across the country in which I (Shannon) have resided (and I've moved quite a bit), the counselors I've known in private practice have followed this transition process.

Clients tend to prefer counselors with backgrounds in schools, agencies, colleges, and other reputable institutions because it provides an endorsement of sorts, so this may provide insight into why most counselors opening their own practice have come from an established career in the schools, agencies, or higher education. Word of mouth still remains a powerful method of advertising, and colleagues in schools, agencies, and universities are more willing to refer clients to professionals with whom they have worked.

Self-employment offers many advantages for counselors in this highly mobile, highly technical age, such as

- being your own boss;
- controlling your own schedule;
- operating with more freedom;
- providing the types of services you enjoy; and
- working on your own schedule.

Self-employment, however, also presents numerous challenges that working for an agency, school, or university does not, including

- absence of employer-paid insurance and retirement benefits;
- inconsistent income;
- in single-shop offices, no in-house coworkers for consultation;
- possible isolation;
- start-up costs;
- advertising;
- billable limitations of insurance companies and sliding-fee scales; and
- competition.

When you work for yourself, you become a one-person operation. You are, effectively, not only the lead counselor, but also the departments of marketing, accounting, technical support, scheduling, and research and development. In practical terms,

- if you need to get the word out about your services, *you* are the one who will put together your marketing or public relations plan—unless you pay someone else to do it for you;
- *you* are the one who gets to figure out how to set up and input information into your accounting software; send invoices to clients; collect fees; wade through endless government forms related to incorporation and taxation at the local, state, and federal levels; and interface with various insurance boards to gain both authorization and reimbursement—unless you pay someone else to do it for you;
- when your computer crashes, you need to upgrade hardware or software, or you need to figure out how to make one phone line operate both a telephone and a fax machine without human intervention, *you* get to deal with it—unless you pay someone else to do it for you;
- *you* will answer the phone and schedule your own appointments—unless you pay someone else to do it for you; and
- in your "spare" time, you can conduct research and develop your own theories and techniques, usually without the benefit of graduate assistants or doctoral fellows—unless you want to pay for one out of your corporate budget.

In this text, *private practice* refers to counseling, but it can also refer to many services besides those considered to be traditional counseling. Personal coaching and mediation services are two examples of services that some counselors provide. Many counselors have found that although personal coaching and mediation do not target psychotherapeutic issues, the skills necessary for such work are similar to those used in counseling, and private practice counselors have been able to develop a revenue stream from clients seeking this type of support.

Private practice may also involve consultation, employee assistance programs (EAPs), psychoeducational workshop presentations (e.g., stress management, test anxiety, managing depression), career counseling, and much more. In fact, if you are going into private practice in today's market, where there is stiff competition from psychiatrists, psychologists, social workers, other counselors, marriage and family therapists, and pastoral counselors, among others, you would be wise to branch out and offer an array of services in which you have adequate training and experience. Although "adequate training" is not explicitly defined in the *ACA Code of Ethics* (American Counseling Association [ACA], 2005), ask yourself whether you would be able to defend the services you offer in a courtroom or at an ethics hearing.

Maslow for Private Practitioners

Every counselor alive has heard of Abraham Maslow and his Hierarchy of Human Needs. Given that a business is treated as an individual, at least in the United States, we thought it would be interesting to present some basic information about starting your own private practice in counseling terms.

Physical Needs

Let's begin with *physical* needs, which are the most basic needs for existence. Although food, water, air, and shelter are basic human needs, in this model we include the most basic professional needs as "physical needs." The reason we have taken the liberty to list these needs as "physical" is simply because minus these, your existence as a private practitioner in counseling is impossible. So, we hope readers will excuse our malapropism involving the use of Maslow's hierarchy, especially regarding physical needs.

Licensure

Your first and foremost need is *licensure*. Check your state's laws to make certain you are in compliance and have secured all the necessary credentials to legally practice your craft. *We cannot stress this enough because if you practice illegally, and are prosecuted for doing so, you may never again be able to practice legally.* In most instances, practicing illegally is also a serious ethics violation. If you aren't already intimately familiar with the licensure laws in your state, get familiar with them quickly. Be aware that many of these laws are in the process of changing, so if you haven't checked in the past year or so, it would be a good idea to ensure that you are still in compliance.

Different states have different standards. Illinois, for example, has two-tiered licensing. The initial license, usually called a licensed professional counselor, or LPC, provides the ability to counsel in a school or agency. The licensed clinical professional counselor credential provides the ability to maintain a private practice, bill insurance, and so forth. Other states allow private practice with the standard LPC or licensed mental health counselor, licensed marriage and family counselor, or a similar credential.

As you have probably ascertained by now, an LPC in one state does not necessarily equate to an LPC in another state. Terms and conditions vary widely as you cross the state borders of this great nation.

To alleviate some of the confusion with the differences in state licensure, the ACA publishes (and updates biennially) a comprehensive manual, *Licensure Requirements for Professional Counselors: A State-by-State Report*, which provides details of licensure, scope of practice, state contacts, and more, for every state in the union. (Parts of this publication are also accessible online to members of ACA at www.counseling.org/Counselors/LicensureAndCert.aspx). If you are contemplating a job search that may necessitate an out-of-state move, or if you are a professor or advisor to counselors who need to find out about licensure portability, this is a highly recommended resource.

Experience

Simply having a license is not enough to successfully begin a practice. Counselors contemplating private practice should have several years experience in counseling and supervising other counselors. What constitutes "enough" experience to pursue this course? Individual differences in life and practice experiences will influence this, but on average, you can esti-mate 2 to 3 years to complete requirements for licensure, then at least the same amount of time practicing with licensure, including 3 to 5 years su-pervising other counselors. So, if you have less than, say, 7 years experience, you may want to reconsider private practice.

A Place to Meet Clients

Will you work out of your home or a separate office? Although working from home means no extra rent and the ability to write off expenses, do you really want clients to know where you live? Depending on your scope of practice, a separate office, shared with other practitioners, may be your best choice. You may also be able to find some creative solutions to space re-quirements. (We know counselors who have space in religious institutions and community centers, for example.) Recognize that maintaining both cli-ent confidentiality and your own boundaries are two basic needs that any space decisions must address.

Furnishings

At a minimum, you'll need a secure place for files, work surfaces, good lighting (especially if you're older than 40!), and comfortable seating for face-to-face meetings with clients.

Communication, Technology, and Tools of the Trade

Yep. *Needs.* Today's business requires communication via e-mail (Internet access) and phone. Computers, telephones, printers, fax machines, and scanners (four-in-one printer–copier–fax–scanners are space and money savers) are tools that are considered basic equipment for today's office.

You'll also need to arrange for access to any assessment tools you'll use in your practice. When you're on your own, the university doesn't pay for those anymore.

Definition of Practice and Establishment of Fees

We debated about where on Maslow's hierarchy this belonged but deter-mined that it's pretty basic to establishing a private practice. You have to be able to communicate what you are able to do for clients and how you will be compensated.

Your professional "scope of competence" will come into play here. *The ACA Code of Ethics* (ACA, 2005) states that counselors must "practice only within the boundaries of their competence" (Standard C.2.a). Although *com-petence* is not operationally defined, it generally implies that the counselor has adequate training and experience to provide the service advertised. For example, if you have a degree or certification in marriage and family counsel-ing and several years providing marriage and relational counseling, you can likely claim to be practicing within your scope of competence. If, however, you have neither training nor experience in marriage and family counseling, advertising and operating as such would suggest you are practicing beyond your scope of competence.

Insurance Boards

Most states now allow licensed counselors to bill for insurance. Also, many counselors charge for services using sliding-fee scales. Remember, counselors who bill for insurance reimbursement must bill sliding-fee clients at the same rate they bill insurance companies. For this reason, and also because HMOs limit sessions to six to eight meetings, many counselors in private practice do not bill insurance. Be aware also that some states still do not allow licensed counselors to bill insurance.

Working Capital

It takes money to make money. Undercapitalization is often cited as the number one reason why small businesses fail.

Do you have enough capital to survive until your practice begins to turn a profit? We have spoken to numerous counselors in private practice, and several have told us it took 1 to 2 years before they began turning a profit. If your spouse or partner has a good-paying job, this nonprofit period may be survivable. But if you have children or a life partner earning only a moderate income or are single and your practice is your sole source of income, you will need to generate enough income to cover your expenses and pay yourself. You'll also need to keep some cash in reserve for unexpected expenses.

The amount of time it takes a new business to become profitable is the reason that many counselors begin their private practice on a part-time basis, keeping their regular jobs until they feel confident in their ability to turn a profit in private practice.

Ethics

Ethics are so intertwined with being a counselor that it is almost redundant to mention them here. Certainly confidentiality and boundaries, previously mentioned, are of primary importance. As you establish a private practice, one element you must address, ethically, is your end-of-practice plan.

What happens to your clients if something happens to you? Who will provide backup if you're on vacation? This issue is addressed in the most recent revision of ACA's (2005) *Code of Ethics*, and if you haven't given it thought, you are ethically obligated to do so.

Safety Issues

Safety, in this context, includes both protecting your physical self and protecting your business entity. How do you protect your practice? And how do you protect yourself?

If your scope of practice includes working with individuals who have been violent—or with those who have been threatened by others—physical safety may be an issue for you to explore. Do you need an alarm system with a panic button? Will good locks on the door to your office provide your clients with an extra sense of security? Or would this feel threatening to them? Does your client assessment take into consideration any special security measures you might need to use?

Legal Protection

As a counseling professional, you know about boundaries. You may determine that you need to put a legal boundary between your personal assets and your business assets. Consult an attorney for assistance on these specific points:

- If you have entered practice with several other counselors, you will want a lawyer to draft specific language outlining specific party responsibilities (Remley & Herlihy, 2007).
- If you are interested in incorporation, an attorney will be best able to advise you as to which type is best suited to your business. The most popular set-ups are S-corps, limited liability corporations, and limited liability partnerships.
- A client agreement, spelling out what services you can and cannot provide and outlining confidentiality and so forth, may be advisable to manage client expectations.

Accounting Systems

Once you have incorporated your business, you'll want to establish a bank account in the name of your business. As a private business, you will need to file quarterly and year-end taxes. Because of the complexity of such, we recommend you engage an accountant who is familiar with small business. These services are tax deductible as a business expense and may be well worth the cost to save yourself the frustration of unfamiliar reports.

If you want to handle your books yourself, then you may, at a minimum, want to seek (*free*) guidance from SCORE (Service Corps of Retired Executives), a government-sponsored organization affiliated with the Small Business Administration. This organization consists of retired executives who act as advisors to small business. Find a local chapter by visiting their Web site, www.score.gov.

Insurance

You may already have liability insurance to cover malpractice, but you'll want to check your policy to make certain it covers your new circumstances. You may also need a policy to cover your office space to insure against damage from fire, theft, and the like. Although many counseling experts advise against using your home as a counseling office because you may not want people to know where you live, if you do this you may consider an umbrella policy. Check with the experts to determine your needs. Remember, one lawsuit, even if unsuccessful, can wipe you out. The bottom line is that you need to get some expert advice regarding insurance and type of coverage.

Protection of Records

Part of maintaining client confidentiality includes the safekeeping of client records. The very basic security includes a locked filing cabinet or password protection for electronic files. You also need to invest in a good antivirus software to prevent intruders from reading or corrupting your data.

Anyone who has ever lived through a hard drive crash will tell you that the experience is less painful if records have been backed up electronically. A number of automatic, online backup systems are available at a reasonable annual cost. The advantage to remote backup is that if your data are lost due to flood or fire, you won't also lose the backup, as you might if the backup disk was stored next to your computer. If you choose to subscribe to one of these services, ask the customer service representative if *they* have redundant systems in case *their* facility is visited by disaster.

Collections

It is very difficult to collect fees from clients who do not pay. You cannot send these clients to collection agencies because this practice constitutes a breach of confidentiality (Remley & Herlihy, 2007). You must also be careful not to terminate such nonpaying clients too soon because this could be a case for client abandonment. Talk the situation over with the client and offer to refer him or her to a public agency or other low-cost provider. Then, document everything you have done in the client's file. Remember, should the case become litigious, documentation is your protection.

Love and Belonging (Establishing Your Reputation)

In this model, we have interpreted loving and belonging as establishing collegial relationships that provide referrals and synergy in the workplace.

Marketing Plan

Once you've taken the steps to establish and protect your business, the next order of business is to build your client base. Do you have a marketing plan? If you don't, you would be wise to develop one. Again, this is where long-term, established counselors moving from schools, agencies, and colleges have an advantage. They are already known in the field. Also, the Web is the 21st-century version of the Yellow Pages. Develop a Web site that introduces you and provides an overview of your credentials, experience, services offered, philosophy, and theoretical approach to counseling. You'll also want to share important contact information: where your office is located, phone numbers, e-mail, and so forth.

Who Loves You, Baby?

As you develop your marketing plan, this is when you tap into your network of contacts. Do you already have a healthy list of referral resources? Or do you need to step up your outreach efforts to gain name recognition and establish a solid reputation in your community? Reach out to physicians, educators, clergy, and fellow counseling professionals who regularly encounter individuals who could benefit from counseling.

Membership Has Its Privileges

Look into the support tools offered by the professional organizations to which you belong. The National Career Development Association (NCDA), for example, offers special membership classifications that include a listing and link on their Web site for referral purposes. Local organizations, such as the Chamber of Commerce or merchant associations, often publish directories for area services.

Networking groups also provide a venue for meeting other professionals and gaining referrals. Check your local business listings, Yellow Pages, Internet, or library to determine which groups meet in your area.

Presentations and Publications

If you want to be regarded as an expert, look for opportunities to get your name into the community. Try writing articles for the local paper, the school newsletter, or the church bulletin. Offer a free presentation on your area of expertise at a library, school, or religious institution in the area. Conduct a workshop at the local bookstore. Host a networking group for job seekers. Once people in your community understand how and whom you can help, you'll start to see the benefits on your calendar and in your checkbook.

Marketing Tools

Back in chapter 1, we presented the Counselor's Marketing Tool Box. Almost any type of business needs a Web site these days, particularly those that are trying to grow. A biography is often a better choice than a résumé for interaction with potential clients and referrals. Business cards and brochures are great leave-behinds to share with colleagues who may provide referrals to you.

Self-Esteem (Professional Reputation)

Your professional reputation will be built on your ability to deliver on services offered. Always remember this maxim when pondering what services to advertise under your banner: Would I feel competent in defending my training, experience, and credentialing should a client sue or report me to the ethics board? All counselors and other mental health clinicians have their professional limitations and need to have a list of professional colleagues for referral purposes.

Identifying the services that are appropriately offered by your practice, then, directly relates to your long-term professional success.

What Services Should I Provide?

This question is more complicated than it appears. Naturally, most counselors plan to provide some type of counseling services, but, as previously mentioned, you need to branch out to make your business viable. Counselors who can offer group, couples, and family counseling will likely draw more business than those who provide only individual counseling. Here are several services for consideration:

- *Individual counseling.* This is the most basic and common counseling service offered in private practice. All private practitioners will likely offer this service.
- *Career counseling and advising.* In our experience, a significant need for good career counseling, advising, and assessment expertise exists.

Given that so many people are unemployed, underemployed, or unhappy with their current job or career, this is an area worth considering. Should you offer career services, make sure you have had extensive experience administering and interpreting popular career search assessments such as the Myers-Briggs Type Inventory (Myers & Myers, 1995), the Strong Interest Inventory (Donnay, Morris, Schaubhut, & Thompson, 2005), Campbell Interests and Skills Survey (Campbell, 2002), or another Holland-based instrument.

- *Mediation and conflict resolution.* A growing number of counselors are trained and certified in mediation and conflict resolution. Mediation has become very popular in certain regions of the United States (Moore, 2003). Many states require a state credentialing process before you can receive court-mandated mediation referrals. Some counselor education programs are now offering graduate training in mediation. Divorce mediation is also popular among marriage and family counselors.
- *EAPs.* Many counselors contract with corporations, school districts, and human services organizations to provide EAPs. EAPs typically allow a set number of sessions for employees (six to eight or so). The counselor would then bill the corporation once services are complete.
- *Couples and family counseling.* In most cases, couples and family counseling is not insurance billable. This opens up opportunity for counselors operating on a sliding-fee scale. The sliding-fee scale usually includes charging uninsured clients on the basis of their monthly income and is a common practice in the counseling field. We recommend that general counselors (those without a marriage and family counseling or therapy degree) take additional training and ongoing supervision with a clinician experienced in marriage and family counseling.
- *Group counseling.* Group counseling was popularized by luminaries such as Fritz and Laura Perls in the 1960s and 1970s. Like marriage and family counseling, group counseling is generally not billable, thus necessitating a sliding-fee scale. Some established counselors may receive court-mandated referrals (e.g., alcohol and drug treatment groups, domestic batterers' intervention) or offer groups through an EAP (described earlier). Types of group services could be standard psychotherapeutic groups, growth groups, support groups, and the like. Although group size varies, most experts recommend that groups be restricted to 8 to 12 members depending on the group (Corey, 2008).
- *Consultation and supervision services.* Counselors and other professionals often provide supervision and consultation for beginning counselors for a fee. Supervision and consultation fees vary greatly depending on the area of the country, urban versus suburban versus rural setting, and the supervisor's reputation. Any counselor offering consultation and supervision services should be licensed and certified and have several years' experience supervising counselors in the workplace.
- *Personal coaching:* Personal coaching has become a very popular service. Counselors are one of the primary professions providing coaching. Should you provide this emerging service, you need to clearly dif-

ferentiate the differences between coaching and counseling, explain precisely how you will provide personal coaching, and enumerate the limitations in confidentiality. Also, clearly explain to the public your qualifications to offer "personal" coaching.

Self-Actualization: Achieving Success in Business

Success in business is never a guarantee. For counselors, there is plenty of competition in the therapeutic marketplace, given all the mental health professionals involved. Starting a small business is also risky—and a private practice *is* a small business; the U.S. Small Business Bureau (2008) has estimated that more than 50% of small businesses fail within the first 5 years.

Entrepreneur Michael Ames (1994, as cited in Remley & Herlihy, 2007, p. 284) offered the following eight reasons for small business failures:

1. Lack of experience
2. Insufficient capital
3. Poor location
4. Poor inventory management
5. Overinvestment in fixed assets
6. Poor credit arrangements
7. Personal use of business funds
8. Unexpected growth

It is not our intention to scare you away from private practice because many counselors are quite successful in this endeavor. We do want you to be aware of the risks involved, however, and understand the huge commitment private practice involves.

Chapter

8

Thriving in Your Career

Thriving. As defined by *Webster's Dictionary* (1992), the word *thrive* means "to prosper or flourish; to be successful, as through good management."

This book is being written during a time of severe economic downturn when much of the world is examining how resources are distributed. *Thrift*, in this era, is an admirable characteristic, defined (again, by *Webster's Dictionary*, 1992) as "frugality, or economical management." The word *thrift* is actually derived from the Middle English word for *thrive*, suggesting that thrift is the path to thriving.

It would follow, then, that thriving in your career will require you to show thrift, that is, to manage your resources effectively. Your time, your intellect, your education, and other personal resources, including financial resources, will be consumed and replenished in the pursuit, and as a result, of your professional goals.

In chapters 1 through 7, we examined the many aspects of managing the job search process to a successful end. When we proposed this book to the American Counseling Association (ACA), one of the items of discussion revolved around professional development. It was clear to everyone involved that although many books, articles, and Web sites provide information on job searching, interviewing, and so forth, there was a paucity of information on development once you get into your career. We recognize career development as an ongoing process that lasts as long as your career.

As counselors, we are required to attain state licensure, compile continuing education (CEs, formerly continuing education units), perhaps become certified in one of the particular counseling specialty areas, write professional journal articles and books (counselor educators), and engage in a number of other career-building activities. Just as in the previous seven chapters in this manual, in this chapter you will be reading *our* platform for career development. We also encourage you to seek out opinions from current and former professors, coworkers, and career counselors and read notable experts such as Richard Nelson Bolles. As always, the place to start is at the beginning.

Managing Your New Job

So, you got the job. What's next? Although completing appropriate academic preparation and applying, interviewing, and negotiating for a great job in your chosen field are all crucial steps in the process of occupational success, these steps are only the beginning of prospering in your career. The thrill of the chase will eventually ebb and flow into a day-to-day routine. Thus, although getting the job you desired was the first step, thriving in your job is, in some ways, a more challenging endeavor. We recommend that you put into building your career the same energy, commitment, and creativity as you put into landing that desired job.

Unlike most corporate entities, few organizations hiring counselors have specific training programs for new employees. Although the human resources department at an accounting firm might follow a 10-step program to welcome new employees (announcing the employee is joining the team, welcoming the employee, setting up a work area and a training schedule, etc.), you may be left to determine your own way forward.

Here, then, are some recommended strategies for starting out on the right foot:

- *Plan your own orientation.* What do you need to know to be effective in your job? Consider everything from creature comforts (Where are the restrooms? What's the coffee policy? [*Note from Shannon:* In two places of employment, the coffee policy caused major conflicts—who paid and who didn't, who's drinking the lion's share, who cleaned up the spills on the counter, etc. People do sweat the small stuff. Tread lightly regarding the coffee policy!] Where do I park? What do people do for lunch?) to administrative functions (Where is the printer? Do I need a code to make copies? How are appointments scheduled?) to the administrative hierarchy (Who holds the real power in the organization? How do things *really* get done here?). Make a list of the questions you need to answer for yourself and set out a plan to begin finding answers, recognizing that some answers will require observation and finesse rather than explicit questioning.

  If your schedule permits, you might stop by your new place of employment a day or two before your first day on the job to handle any administrative tasks related to your employment and to prepare your office, if it is available, so you're ready to hit the ground running on Day 1. (Call ahead to make certain that you won't be disrupting others' schedules.)

- *Keep interviewing—with your new colleagues, that is.* You're the new kid on the block, and everyone will be watching you. Now is the time to establish yourself as the professional you hinted at during your interview process. The routines you demonstrate during your first 90 days on the job will formulate your colleagues' expectations of you. Are you on time and prepared for meetings, or do you slouch and seem disinterested? Here's some advice: Be on time for meetings, be well groomed, appear interested (even if the agenda is dullsville, do not act bored), and bring material to take notes. Meetings are public forums at which coworkers will be evaluating new hires, and you want to create the right impression. Be intentional in the image you wish to create of yourself. Also, do you follow through on the projects you've assumed, or do the boss and your coworkers have to prod you? Do you return phone calls and e-mails in a timely fashion? Are you proving yourself to be a leader on specific initiatives? Do you have regular input regarding new endeavors and initiatives? Now, regarding the last point, give input, but as a new hire, give it judiciously, as long-time staff and faculty may resent new staff who seem to know it all.

- *Be prepared to "go with the flow."* Although it's a good idea to be prepared to orient yourself, it's possible that someone else has already taken on the task of prepping you. If this occurs, follow the prescribed program, but check it against your own plan to make sure all of your questions are answered. You will also need to be strategic regarding dissent. Schools, universities, and agencies hire highly educated, experienced counselors for their knowledge, not to be cyborgs who merely state the party line. But we would be remiss if we did not state that some long-time staff and faculty may be threatened by new hires. So, pick the battles you fight when you are new. (*Note:* We consider "new" counseling staff to be anyone who has been in his or her current job for less than 1 year.) New staff should also cultivate mentors and seek out their advice when controversial issues arise.

- *Request feedback.* True professionals are open to constructive criticism. If a formal evaluation isn't part of your orientation or probation period, then ask your supervisor for an informal check-in. Not sure what to say? Try something like "Now that I've been here for a few months, I wonder whether you might have some time to discuss my progress in becoming part of this staff." If you have some specific areas of concern, you might mention them here, as well. Ask, "What can I do to improve?" In our experience, most staff do not actively seek out advice regarding improvement, and willingness to do so may pay off. But once again, remember to be strategic: Seek out feedback on how to improve, but don't do it too often or else you risk sending the message that you lack confidence.

- *Play well with others.* Remember, the most common reason why people lose their job or leave their job is because of conflicts with coworkers (Bolles, 2004). So, although your counselor education program trained you well; although you may be licensed or certified, with several years of experience; and although, for counselor educators, you may be a graduate of a Council for Accreditation of Counseling and

Related Educational Programs (CACREP) doctoral program and have numerous publications, it's your people skills that may enhance or derail your counseling career. When you do have conflicts, seek to resolve them with the individual, rather than triangulating with third parties. Although office gossip is a reality, steer as clear as you can of it because repeating malicious rumors could be a firing offense. (Try to be aware, though, of what is floating through the office. Knowing what is hanging on the grapevine can be beneficial in avoiding political pitfalls. "Ears open, mouth shut" is a good mantra.)

- In agencies, schools, hospitals, and counselor education departments, it pays to be your own personal ombudsman regarding conflict resolution. When you have conflicts—and you will because you are human—resolve them promptly. In our experience, most people struggle with resolving conflicts. Shannon, ever the good cognitive counselor, suggests you practice resolving a conflict with a friend, coworker, or spouse before attempting an actual resolution. Practice will help you carry out resolving a conflict and may take the edge off any animus you may have built up toward a particular coworker.

Managing Licensure Issues

In the profession of counseling, the primary credential to work toward is state licensure. We'll reiterate here what we know you have heard numerous times from your counselor education faculty or clinical supervisor: Achieving licensure at the earliest possible time is very important!

Nearly every state has three elements (also known as "the three Es") of licensure: education, examination, and experience:

1. *Education* refers to the hours of graduate study you have completed in pursuit of a master's or doctoral degree. The "gold standard" is a 60-hour master's degree from a CACREP-accredited program, which will ensure that you will meet the current minimum academic requirement for licensure in all states.
2. *Examination* refers to successful completion of a professional competency examination, such as the National Counselor Examination (NCE), the National Clinical Mental Health Counselor Examination (NCMHCE), or another examination designated by the individual state. Remember, states vary regarding which exam is required for licensure. A few, Texas for example, have their own licensure exam.
3. *Experience* refers to supervised experience, better known among insiders simply as "supervision."

When you review the licensure law in your state, be aware that there are two types of law: title law, in which only licensed counselors can carry the title of counselor and advertise as such, and scope-of-practice law, which means you cannot practice counseling (which often includes a detailed and specific list) without a license.

States such as New York, where counseling falls under both a title law and a scope of practice law, often have a temporary license or certificate for practice until you have completed all requirements for general licensure. In the Internet age, state licensure boards provide information online, making information access readily available. Currently, 49 states; Washington, DC; Puerto Rico; and Guam license counselors. The lone state without a generic counselor licensure law is California, but a proposal to create counselor licensure is currently working its way through the state legislature.

Regardless of what happens with the current licensure initiative in California, there is an expectation in the counseling profession that in the near future, all 50 states and territories will have achieved this critical professional watermark.

If you plan to seek employment straight out of your graduate program, you will need to apply for and receive a temporary license in any state that requires a license to provide counseling services. There are differences that make the licensure situation somewhat complex. State licensure requirements vary, although most require a minimum of 48 semester or 72 quarter credits or, in more recent cases, 60 semester hours or 90 quarter credits. Some states license mental health counselors, marriage and family counselors, and creative arts counselors, but not school counselors. In other states, counselors are required to be state certified as opposed to licensed. ACA's (2008) publication *Licensure Requirements for Professional Counselors: A State-by-State Report* is updated biennially and provides comprehensive information on requirements for licensure in each state and details regarding title and practice limitations.

Whatever counseling specialty area you are going into, check your particular state's requirements. Some states require counselors to achieve 3,000 post-master's-degree supervised clock hours before allowing them to sit for the state licensure examination, and others require only 1,000 or 2,000 post-master's-degree clock hours. Not all of the 49 states require you to be licensed to provide counseling services. But even if you reside in a state that does not require you to be licensed, we still recommend you achieve licensure as soon as possible.

Licensure Portability

Sometimes inaccurately referred to as "reciprocity," licensure portability refers to those measures you should undertake to ensure that you will be able to practice as a counselor in any of the United States where you may reside.

In recent years, a new initiative, the National Counselor Registry, has been undertaken for the profession by the American Association of State Counseling Boards (AASCB) to develop a national registry for counselors in which counselors can, for a fee, register and store their credentials to support their long-term licensure portability.

You might ask, "Why would I need to do that?" Well, consider for a moment the steps required to obtain licensure. Now, imagine that 20 years from now, you relocate to another state and must prove that you have fulfilled all of the requirements (education, examination, and experience) to become licensed in that state to practice. Although transcripts can be ordered to prove you've completed the academic requirements, test scores and affidavits of supervision may not be as easy to obtain. Supervisors move away; some may even have passed away. Registering your credentials through this program ensures that they will be available when you need them and should make licensure portability easier through classification of your credentials.

At the present time, half of U.S. states have completed the regulatory changes necessary to effectively use this service, are in the process of doing so, or have indicated support for the program and intend to begin the legislation process. For up-to-date information about this program, you can consult the AASCB's Web site (www.aascb.org). You will also be able to download forms to register your credentials through this Web site.

Licensure is important because as a counselor, you want to be able to demonstrate to clients, colleagues, and the general public that you have met the gold standard in your field, and licensure helps you achieve that. Licensure also strengthens the profession because it demonstrates a commitment to high standards, and it protects the public by announcing that said licensed counselor is indeed a qualified mental health professional.

Once you complete your counseling program, it's helpful to begin actively studying for the licensure exam, even though, depending on the state, it may be 2 years away. There are many counselor study guides available. Perusing *Counseling Today*, the monthly magazine published by the ACA, will reveal several study guides prominently advertised. We suggest you order one of these and immediately begin studying for the licensure examination.

Most counselors practicing in agency settings or private practice will be taking the NCMHCE, although some will take the NCE; a few states, such as Texas, have developed their own examination. Although it is difficult to say with precision how long a counselor should study for the licensure exam, Shannon recommends a minimum of 6 months. Regardless of which exam you are required to take, it's important to be prepared and to pass it at the earliest possible time. Studying in pairs or groups is ideal because it provides encouragement and accountability, provided such is practical. Scheduling 2 evenings per week for 2 hours of study over a 6-month period also means it's more likely you will commit to the process as opposed to a vague goal of weekly studying.

Obtaining Supervision

The issue of licensure also makes supervision a critical issue. When interviewing for counseling positions, be sure to inquire about clinical supervision. (You can request a list of approved supervisors through your state licensure authority.)

For counselor licensure, most states will require supervision from a licensed counselor, social worker, psychologist, or marriage and family therapist. Before you accept a counseling job, make sure that your supervisor of record is licensed. When possible, we suggest contacting your state's licensure authority with your supervision plan and having it approved, in writing, before proceeding. Supervision from a licensed counselor is most helpful because a colleague from this profession will better understand and is far more likely to support the profession than are other mental health professionals such as social workers and psychologists.

As a newly hired counselor, you will have little say about the person providing your supervision. Exceptions to this exist because some agencies will allow the counselor some voice in choosing a supervisor. The supervisor's most important function is to provide good clinical oversight, to help continue the new counselor's professional growth, and to mentor a new mental health professional.

Good clinical supervisors also establish two-way communication whereby the supervisee can provide feedback on what has been helpful in the supervisor–supervisee relationship. In the event a counselor has been hired in a remote region where supervision is not an easy option, the ACA and many of its state affiliates provide a supervision referral service. Should you work in a remote area and need outside supervision, we recommend you negotiate to have your agency or school pay for this service.

If you need suggestions on choosing a supervisor, state counseling organizations often have lists of potential supervisors. Supervision rates vary depending on the area, although you can expect to pay anywhere from $25 to $60 an hour. Thus, supervision can be very expensive indeed, but you should consider it a necessary cost of completing your education and meeting your career goals.

Be aware, also, that one day you are likely to be providing the supervision for a beginning counselor. When your day as a supervisor arrives, remember what was helpful and less helpful when you were the supervisee. Remember that you are mentoring a newly minted counseling professional and that this is weighty responsibility. Actively solicit input from the supervisee, and when tension occurs, deal with it immediately but with a gentle hand. Many counselor supervisors with whom we have spoken say that the supervisory role was the catalyst for the greatest professional growth in their careers.

Managing Your Credentials

Once you have attained licensure, it may be beneficial to pursue additional training and certification in specific applications of counseling technique. Following are several examples of possible continued study.

Certification

In an era when state licensure was in its infancy, the National Board for Certified Counselors (NBCC), an independent, nonprofit credentialing body, was created from an ACA committee to provide the counseling field a national standard and credential (Remley & Herlihy, 2007). In the current era, in which only California lacks counselor licensure, certification has emerged as a credential for specialists in counseling.

NBCC's flagship credential is the National Certified Counselor (NCC), which is probably the most common. NBCC now offers specialty certification in three areas:

1. School counseling: the National Certified School Counselor (NCSC)
2. Clinical mental health counseling: the Certified Clinical Mental Health Counselor (CCMHC)
3. Addictions counseling: the Master Addictions Counselor

In addition to these three specialty areas, NBCC also offers the Approved Clinical Supervisor for counseling supervisors and counselor educators.

One of the questions new counselors are likely to ask is "Do I need to obtain the national certification?" The most immediate answer is "no." Licensure is the credential that is most important to a counselor's career. But national certification is emerging as a specialty area in counseling, much in the way it has in medicine. For example, your doctor is state licensed (or better be!) but may hold an additional board-certified credential in, say, orthopedics. For counselors, although certification in a specialty is voluntary, it can be advantageous to secure appropriate specialty certifications. So, obtain your counselor license (Licensed Professional Counselor [LPC] or Licensed Mental Health Counselor [LMHC]) and national certification (NCC, CCMHC, Approved Clinical Supervisor [ACS]).

Some critics may argue that certification is an unnecessary expense in the age of licensure, but in our field extras count, and the national certification is not particularly expensive. So, our position is that you strongly consider obtaining the national certification.

All but a few states have adopted either the NCE leading to the NCC credential or the NCMHCE leading to the CCMHC. Passage of the state licensure exam (with the exceptions previously mentioned) would also allow for a counselor to hold one of the aforementioned national certifications (e.g., NCC, CCMHC).

Alternative Credentials

We need to mention an alternative credentialing process with which many readers of this text may be familiar. Many states will require school counselors, for example, to be state certified as opposed to licensed.

To illustrate, in New York school counselors are not licensed but certified, and currently no exam for state certification exists. Provisional certification can be obtained when a school counselor completes his or her master's degree in school counseling. Once that is achieved, a school counselor has 5 years to complete requirements for permanent certification.

Permanent certification in New York requires 2 years as a full-time school counselor in a public setting and completion of 60 semester credits of graduate counseling courses. Again, check your state's licensure and certification requirements to see what credential you will be working toward.

Another type of credential many counselors earn is the Certified Specialist in Addiction Counseling (CASC). Many addiction counselors may already be CASC-certified before entering a graduate counseling program. Others who have no previous experience in addictions counseling may be supervised for the CASC credential concurrently with supervision for licensure.

Addictions counseling is evolving as a profession. Until recently, addictions counselors predominantly had a personal background in addiction recovery and generally had to prove sobriety of 3 to 5 years, and many had a bachelor's degree or less. Today, addictions counseling appears to be moving toward higher credentials, with the field now embracing master's-degree training. Baccalaureate degree addiction counselors still seem to outnumber master's-level addictions counselors, but this deficit is narrowing. It is also worth mentioning that for counselors hoping to move into supervisory or management positions, the master's degree is typically a requirement.

Continuing Education (CEs)

Most states require counselors to generate a set number of continuing education hours, or CEs (formerly called continuing education units), to maintain licensure, and relevance is behind this requirement. Even though the primary motivation for some counselors to pursue continuing education is maintaining a license, staying current in the field is the only way to continue to be relevant as a professional.

The NBCC (2009) mandates that nationally certified counselors take a minimum number of continuing education hours. NBCC and most states require 100 continuing education hours in a 5-year period. A number of venues for accessing CEs include the ACA (through its Web site, e-courses, journals, and *Counseling Today*); continuing education programs delivered by colleges and universities (note that you should make sure the course offered has approval from NBCC to offer CEs); and private practitioners, who offer training in urban regions around the United States and Canada. Once again, look to see whether the advertised training has been approved by the NBCC. Some institutions will even offer 2-week training (or ongoing training requiring 6 months to 1 year) for certification in a variety of areas: trauma counseling, art therapy, dance therapy, autism spectrum disorders, hypnosis, solution-focused therapy, and many other important mental health topics.

Consultation

After you have completed your supervised clock hours and passed the licensure exam, it is highly likely that you will feel a sense of relief at having completed 6 to 8 years of college and graduate school and 2 years of full-time work with supervision and at having passed a challenging examination. Now that you have reached a plateau, the next stage in lifelong education commences. Your next step in continuing professional education is to establish ongoing consultation with a colleague or supervisor.

As a young clinical supervisor, I (Shannon) was involved in consultation group with four other clinical supervisors. We met every 2 weeks and staffed cases, provided critique and concrete suggestions, watched videos of well-known counseling professionals, and reported on trainings and workshops we had attended. Occasionally, we even read through psychology and counseling texts together and quizzed one another on central points of each text. The consultation group also provided an ongoing support group for professional and even personal issues that arose. Consultation groups also create the opportunity for professional networking because counselors will know counselor supervisors and managers. Whether in a group or one on one, becoming involved in professional consultation is an active method to support your own continued professional growth.

Professional Activism

As a working professional counselor or counselor educator, part of your ongoing development is becoming involved in professional associations. Many counselors complete their graduate education and move into the professional practice arena with little or no involvement in the professional associations that support the field of counseling.

The counseling profession has been able to move forward with licensure, third-party insurance payment, and a stronger voice in state and federal government as a result of professional advocacy by the ACA, the American School Counselor Association (ASCA), the American Mental Heath Counselors Association (AMHCA), and others. We would argue that the strongest professions also have a large central organization that serves as the flagship, as evidenced by the American Psychological Association, the American Medical Association, and the American Chemical Society, for example. All of these professional organizations have divisions within their framework, but the primary organization (e.g., the American Psychological Association [APA]) remains the focus. For our profession of counseling, that flagship organization is ACA. The larger the membership in ACA and its divisional affiliates is, the stronger the lobby at the state and federal level. Thus, we recommend you join ACA *and* your respective division (e.g., ASCA, AMHCA, American Rehabilitation Counseling Association [ARCA]).

Membership in a professional organization such as ACA also means you are connected to a larger body of colleagues involved in the same type of work as you. Professional memberships also pay dividends through professional journals (*Journal of Counseling & Development*), monthly newsletters or magazines (e.g., *Counseling Today*), an interactive Web site, contacts, professional liability insurance, annual and biannual conferences, and many other tangible and intangible benefits.

As mentioned previously in this text, readers will be getting our bias regarding résumés and curricula vitae, cover letters, interviewing techniques, and so forth. The same holds true for professional development. Given the number of national, state, and local organizations, the issue of membership is likely confusing to new counselors. In this section, we attempt to provide clarity to the "alphabet soup" of membership. We have listed several professional organizations that represent the counseling profession. A complete list with Web site addresses is available in the Appendix.

American Counseling Association

ACA is the flagship organization for the counseling profession. ACA has its roots in the 1952 founding of the American Personnel and Guidance Association (APGA). In the nearly 6 decades that have followed, ACA has undergone much evolution regarding its name, membership base, focus, and the services it provides. ACA offers an annual spring conference, the *Journal of Counseling & Development*, the monthly magazine *Counseling Today*, a Web site (www.counseling.org), the *ACA Code of Ethics*, and numerous additional services. We recommend that all professional counselors, regardless of whether they are counselors in schools, public or private agencies, or universities, join and support ACA. Our own opinion is that all professionals benefit from a strong centralized organization, and ACA as the largest counseling organization in the world represents unity. ACA also lobbies Congress for legislation that strengthens the profession and each counselor's professional rights. Each state also has an ACA state affiliate organization. Check with ACA for your state affiliate counseling organization.

Divisional Affiliates

ACA also has 19 divisional affiliates (as of 2009). A complete list can be found in the Appendix, so we won't list all of them here. Divisional affiliate organizations are narrower in scope than ACA and represent specialty areas of the counseling profession. Some affiliates, such as ASCA and AMHCA, are divisions of ACA but operate autonomously. We do also recommend you join your affiliate division (ASCA, ARCA, AMHCA, etc.) in addition to holding membership in ACA. We list a few of the more notable affiliate organizations here.

American School Counselor Association

ASCA is the divisional affiliate organization for school counseling. ASCA has been very instrumental in promoting reforms to the school counseling profession (see the ASCA National Model at www.schoolcounselor. org). ASCA also offers a professional journal (*Professional School Counseling*), monthly newsletter, and numerous other services. ASCA also offers their professional conference with ACA. We recommend all school counselors join ASCA in addition to ACA.

American Mental Health Counselors Association

AMHCA (www.amhca.org) is the divisional affiliate representing the profession of mental health counseling. AMHCA publishes a professional journal (*Journal of Mental Health Counseling*) and a monthly newsletter, and a separate national conference is held in the summer. If you are a mental health counselor, we recommend you join both ACA and AMHCA.

American Rehabilitation Counseling Association

ARCA (www.arcaweb.org) represents rehabilitation counseling. ARCA also has a separate journal and newsletter. If you are a rehabilitation counselor and are not currently a member of ARCA, we encourage you to join.

Association of Counselor Education and Supervision

The Association of Counselor Education and Supervision (ACES; www. acesonline.net) is a broad organization representing counselor educators teaching in universities and counselors supervising in schools, agencies, hospitals, and the military. ACES publishes a journal (*Journal of Counselor Education and Supervision*), maintains an electronic mailing list, and holds affiliate regional conferences. All counselor education professors would be advised to join ACES in addition to ACA.

American College Counseling Association

The American College Counseling Association (ACCA; www.college counseling.org/) is the one unified, national organization representing college and university counseling. ACCA also publishes a journal (*Journal of College Counseling*) and a newsletter and holds a biannual conference. ACCA membership is open to counselors in traditional 4-year institutions and in 2-year technical and community college counseling centers.

Future of Counseling

As we wrote in chapter 1, counseling is the fastest growing of the mental health professions (U.S. Department of Labor, 2008). Although there are challenges for the counseling profession to overcome (licensure in all 50 states and territories, third-party billing in all states, and the ability to bill Medicare, to name the major ones), the profession has emerged from its infancy into early adulthood.

Everyone reading this text needs to become professionally active to create a stronger, more visible, more diverse global organization. As we have written throughout this text, we strongly recommend that you join ACA and divisions that correlate with your specialty area (e.g., ASCA, AMHCA). Your membership helps to support advocacy efforts and outreach and creates a more sustainable profession. Professional counseling organizations provide important advocacy that strengthens the profession and protects your right to practice. If it were not for ACA, ASCA, AMHCA, and so forth, there would be no state licensure. Professional membership is an investment in the future of counseling.

One of the most significant collaborations between the various counseling divisions and disciplines is *20/20: A Vision for the Future of Counseling*. This major initiative is cosponsored by the ACA and the American Association of State Counseling Boards (AASCB). Thirty counseling organizations are represented in this effort to proactively plan for the future of our profession.

In 2008, the 30 organizations approved seven *Principles for Unifying and Strengthening the Profession*:

1. Sharing a common professional identity
2. Presenting ourselves as a united profession
3. Working together to improve public perception of counseling and to advocate for professional issues related to counseling
4. Creating a portability system for licensure that will make it easier for reciprocity for counselors moving from one state to another
5. Expanding and promoting our research base
6. Focusing on students and prospective students to ensure the ongoing health of the counseling profession

7. Promoting client welfare and advocacy for the populations we serve (ACA, n.d.)

We mention the 20/20 initiative because not only it is important for you to find a counseling job, but it is equally important that your career, and the professions that support your career, remain healthy, viable, and able to adapt to the groundswell of change represented by a dynamic, global mental health field. Some of you reading this text hold citizenship in a country other than the United States. Although the international counseling profession is small, it is growing and likely to be a major focus in the next decade. Many of you will have counseling careers or provide counselor education overseas. The 20/20 endeavor is a comprehensive effort to lay the foundation for a successful future.

Managing Your Ongoing Career

Words are powerful, and they are meaningful. Take the word *professional* as an example. What image does that word create for you? The field of counseling is a profession, but to be professional, you must exhibit certain characteristics. Foremost are displaying reliability and dependability to your clients and your colleagues. Enthusiasm, positivity, resourcefulness, and adaptability are others. You can earn the title licensed professional counselor, but you must make a conscious effort to live out this professionalism.

Pursuing additional certifications and engaging in other professional development activities are all well and good. These activities enhance your own credibility and help to advocate for the profession. But the bottom line is to do your job and to do it well.

If your mission, as defined by your employer, is to spend 50% of your time engaged in professional development activities—and it may well be if you are the chair of a counselor education program attempting to establish itself as the gold standard in counselor preparation—then that is what you should do. But if your mission is to see clients, to run programs, and to teach courses and if your income depends on face-to-face counseling, delivery of workshops, and teaching classes, then the focus of your professional development activities should consist of continuous process improvement in the areas that are most closely aligned with your professional development. When your personal and professional goals are properly aligned with the mission of your position, you have achieved a good fit in your career. This is when you will thrive.

Remember also that not only do you represent yourself as an individual, but you are an emissary of the counseling profession. As you honor yourself, you honor the profession of counseling. (The reverse of this statement is also true.) As you gain experience and move up the ladder of responsibility, we encourage you to remain active in professional organizations and to take the time to mentor new counseling professionals in graduate counseling programs in the schools, agencies, hospitals, and colleges and universities. All of you have something to contribute to our field.

Live well and prosper in your counseling careers!

Appendix

Career Counseling Resources

Web Sites of Professional Counseling Organizations

American College Counseling Association

The American College Counseling Association (ACCA) is the primary professional organization for college and university counseling professionals. It is also open to counseling professionals in psychology and social work.

http://www.collegecounseling.org/

American Counseling Association and Its Divisions (as of 2009)

The American Counseling Association (ACA) is the flagship organization for the counseling profession. ACA's membership is around 42,000. ACA also has 19 chartered divisions providing specific advocacy and information related to the counseling career you have chosen.

www.counseling.org

American Mental Health Counselors Association

The American Mental Health Counselors Association (AMHCA) represents the profession of mental health counseling. Although AMHCA is a division of ACA, it also operates as a separate organization.

www.amhca.org

American Rehabilitation Counseling Association

The American Rehabilitation Counseling Association (ARCA) represents counselor educators, rehabilitation counselors, and students.

www.arcaweb.org

American School Counselor Association

The American School Counselor Association (ASCA) promotes the profession of school counseling. Although ASCA is an ACA affiliate, it also operates as a separate organization from ACA.

www.schoolcounselor.org

Association for Adult Development and Aging

The Association for Adult Development and Aging (AADA) serves as a focal point for professional development and support for counselors working with geriatric populations.

http://www.aadaweb.org/

Association for Assessment in Counseling and Education

The Association for Assessment in Counseling and Education (AACE) promotes the effective use of assessment (testing) in counseling and education.

www.theaaceonline.com/

Association for Counselor Education and Supervision

The Association for Counselor Education and Supervision (ACES) emphasizes the need for quality counselor education and supervision. Counselor educators teaching in the university setting should definitely join ACES.

www.acesonline.net

Association for Counselors and Educators in Government

The Association for Counselors and Educators in Government (ACEG) is dedicated to counseling concerns regarding state, federal, and military settings.

http://www.dantes.doded.mil/dantes_web/organizations/aceg/index.htm

Association for Creativity in Counseling

The Association for Creativity in Counseling (ACC) provides an organization for creative arts counseling and novel counseling approaches.

www.creativecounselor.org

Association for Lesbian, Gay, Bisexual, and Transgender Issues in Counseling

The Association for Lesbian, Gay, Bisexual, and Transgender Issues in Counseling (ALGBTIC) educates counselors in the needs of lesbian, gay, bisexual, and transgender clients.

www.algbtic.org

Association for Multicultural Counseling and Development

The Association for Multicultural Counseling and Development (AMCD) strives to improve the understanding of multicultural issues in counseling.

www.amcdaca.org/amcd/default.cfm

Association for Specialists in Group Work

The Association for Specialists in Group Work (ASGW) provides professional leadership in the field of group counseling.

www.asgw.org

Association for Spiritual, Ethical, and Religious Values in Counseling

The Association for Spiritual, Ethical, and Religious Values in Counseling (ASERVIC) is devoted to addressing spiritual and religious issues in counseling.

www.aservic.org

Counseling Association for Humanistic Education and Development

The Counseling Association for Humanistic Education and Development (C-AHEAD) provides a forum for information on humanistic-oriented counseling practices.

www.c-ahead.org

Counselors for Social Justice

Counselors for Social Justice (CSJ) is committed to equality on a broad array of social issues.

www.counselorsforsocialjustice.com

International Association for Counselling

The International Association for Counselling (IAC) is an international affiliate professional organization to promote the exchange of global counseling information.

www.iac.coe.uga.edu/index.html

International Association of Addictions and Offender Counselors

The International Association of Addictions and Offender Counselors (IAAOC) advocates for the development of effective practice in substance abuse treatment, juvenile offenders, and correctional populations.

www.iaaoc.org

International Association of Marriage and Family Counselors

The International Association of Marriage and Family Counselors (IAMFC) addresses couples and family approaches in counseling.

www.iamfc.org

National Career Development Association

The National Career Development Association's (NCDA's) mission is to promote career development for all.

http://associationdatabase.com/aws/NCDA/pt/sp/Home_Page

National Employment Counseling Association

The National Employment Counseling Association's (NECA's) charge is professional leadership for counselors in career development settings.

www.employmentcounseling.org/

Top Job Boards

At time of publication, counseling positions can be located on these online job boards:

- www.bestjobsusa.com
- www.career.com
- www.careerbuilder.com

- www.careershop.com
- www.careersite.com
- www.coolworks.com
- www.employmentspot.com
- www.4jobs.com
- www.higheredjobs.com
- www.hiregate.com
- www.hotjobs.com
- www.indeed.com
- www.jobbank.com
- www.jobfind.com
- www.jobsearch.org
- www.jobwearhouse.com
- www.monster.com
- www.preferredjobs.com
- www.topjobs.com
- www.truecareers.com

Additional Sources for Occupational Information

In addition to the job boards listed here, check Web sites for local school districts, universities, and so forth.

- www.ajb.dni.us; maintained by the U.S. Department of Labor, links 2,000 state employment services offices
- www.careerbuilder.com; features some 30,000 ads from major news-papers in the United States
- www.monstertrak.com; lists more than 2,000 new job postings each day and also has a free search agent called "Swoop"
- www.careersonline.com.au/col/AskCOL.html; offers bilingual career aptitude testing, career design seminars, job search advising, résumé preparation, and career advising
- www.cooljobs.com; lists "cool" positions
- www.jist.com; provides free job search information
- www.bls.gov; provides the latest U.S. government figures regarding employment trends
- www.bls.gov/oco; includes salary trends and the U.S. Department of Labor, Bureau of Labor Statistic's (2008) *Occupational Outlook Handbook*
- www.workforce.com; deals with employee and legal issues
- www.thechronicle.com; lists faculty, administrative, and student af-fairs positions; the major employment listing for higher education in the United States and abroad
- www.counselingtoday.org; the American Counseling Association's official monthly magazine; also lists job advertisements
- www.higheredjobs.com; lists faculty and professional staff openings in colleges and universities worldwide.

Additional Texts to Consult for Career Assistance

Much additional career information exists for professional counselors. We have included here a list of resources that we have found helpful.

Although not all of these texts are targeted specifically to counselors, we have found that they do have good general career information. Determining what's helpful is an inexact process. Although we have found these resources helpful in our professional journey, we naturally encourage you solicit additional resources from knowledgeable professors, colleagues, and friends.

American Counseling Association. (2008). *Licensure requirements for professional counselors: A state-by-state report*. Alexandria, VA: Author.

Bolles, R. N. (2008). *What color is your parachute?* Berkeley, CA: Ten Speed Press.

Capacchione, L. (2000). *Visioning: Ten steps to designing the life of your dreams*. New York: Tarcher/Putnam.

Collison, B. B., & Garfield, N. (Eds.). (2007). *Careers in counseling and human services* (2nd ed.). New York: Taylor & Francis.

Darley, J. M., Zanna, M. P., & Roediger, H., III. (2007). *The complete academic: A career guide*. Washington, DC: American Psychological Association.

Eneland, W. S., & Kursmark, L. M. (2007). *Cover letter magic: Trade secrets of professional résumé writers*. Indianapolis: JIST Works.

Gysbers, N. C., Heppner, M. J., & Johnson, J. A. (2009). *Career counseling: Contexts, processes, and techniques* (3rd ed.). Alexandria, VA: American Counseling Association.

Janda, L. (1999). *Career tests: 25 revealing self-tests to help you find and succeed at the perfect career*. Avon, MA: Adams Media.

Johnston, S. M. (2001). *The career adventure: Your guide to personal assessment, career exploration, and decision making* (3rd ed.). Upper Saddle River, NJ: Prentice-Hall.

Krannich, R. (2004). *Change your job, change your life: High impact strategies for finding great jobs in the 21st century* (9th ed.). Atascadero, CA: Impact.

Lasley, M. (2004). *Courageous visions: How to unleash passionate energy in your life and your organization*. Burlington, PA: Discover Press.

Parker, Y. (2002). *The damn good résumé guide: A crash course in résumé writing*. Berkeley, CA: Ten Speed Press.

Sinetar, M. (1989). *Do what you love, the money will follow*. Mahwah, NJ: Paulist Press.

Sinetar, M. (1995). *To build the life you want, create the work you love*. New York: St. Martin's Press.

Walsh, R. J., & Dasenbrook, N. D. (2009). *The complete guide to private practice for licensed mental health professionals* (4th ed.). Rockford, IL: Crysand Press.

Yate, M. (2007). *Knock'em dead 2007: The ultimate job search guide*. Avon, MA: Adams Media.

References

American Counseling Association. (2005). *ACA code of ethics*. Alexandria, VA: Author.

American Counseling Association. (2008). *Licensure requirements for professional counselors: A state-by-state report*. Alexandria, VA: Author.

American Counseling Association. (n.d.). *20/20: A vision for the future of counseling*. Retrieved from http://www.counseling.org/20-20/index.aspx

American Mental Health Counselors Association. (2008). *About AMHCA*. Retrieved July 29, 2008, from http://www.amhca.org/about

American Rehabilitation Counseling Association. (2009). *Careers in vocational rehabilitation*. Retrieved July 28, 2009, from http://ncrtm.org/course/view.php?id=7

American School Counselor Association. (2009). *Careers/roles*. Retrieved July 29, 2009, from http://www.schoolcounselor.org/content.asp?pl=325&sl=133&contentid=133

Archer, J., & Cooper, S. (1998). *Counseling and mental services on campus: A handbook of contemporary practices and challenges*. San Francisco: Jossey-Bass.

Arthur, N., & Pedersen, P. (2008). *Case incidents in counseling for international transitions*. Alexandria, VA: American Counseling Association.

Becker, H. A. (1980/1999). The assertive job hunting survey. In L. Janda, *Career tests: 25 revealing self-tests to help you find and succeed at the perfect career* (pp. 113–117). Avon, MA: Adams Media. (Reprinted from *Measurement and Evaluation Guidance, 13,* 43–48, by H. A. Becker, 1980)

Best jobs in America—CNNmoney.com/Money Magazine report. (2006). Retrieved July 24, 2009, from http://www.careerproplus.com/company/article_top_joblist_best_jobs_in_america.php

Bolles, R. N. (1978). *The three boxes of life and how to get out of them.* Berkeley, CA: Ten Speed Press.

Bolles, R. N. (2004). *What color is your parachute? 2005: A practical manual for job-hunters and career-changers.* Berkeley, CA: Ten Speed Press.

Bolles, R. N. (2007). *What color is your parachute? 2008: A practical manual for job-hunters and career-changers.* Berkeley, CA: Ten Speed Press.

Campbell, D. P. (2002). The history and development of the Campbell Interest and Skill Survey. *Journal of Career Assessment, 10,* 150–168.

Capacchione, L. (2000). *Visioning: Ten steps to designing the life of your dreams.* New York: Tarcher/Putnam.

Carnegie, D. (1981). *How to win friends and influence people.* New York: Simon & Schuster.

Chodron, P. (1997). *When things fall apart: Heart advice for difficult times.* Boston: Shambhala.

Corey, G. (2008). *Theory and practice of group counseling* (7th ed.). Belmont, CA: Brooks/Cole.

Covey, S. (1996). *The seven habits of highly effective people.* New York: Simon & Schuster.

Davis, D. C., & Humphrey, K. M. (2000). *College counseling: Issues and strategies for a new millennium.* Alexandria, VA: American Counseling Association.

Donnay, D. A. C., Morris, M. L., Schaubhut, N. A., & Thompson, R. C. (2005). *Strong Interest Inventory manual: Research, development, and strategies for interpretation.* Mountain View, CA: CPP.

Ellis, A. E. (1994). *Reason and emotion in psychotherapy revised.* New York: Kensington.

Ellis, D. (2008). *Life coaching: A manual for helping professionals.* Bethel, CT: Crown House Publications.

Gallagher, R. P. (2007). *National survey of college center directors* (Monograph Series No. 8Q). Alexandria, VA: International Association of Counseling Services. Retrieved July 12, 2008, from http://www.iacsinc.org/Nsccd-SurveyFinal_v2.pdf

Goleman, D. (1995). *Emotional intelligence.* New York: Bantam.

Gray, P., & Drew, D. E. (2008). *What they didn't teach you in graduate school: 199 helpful hints for success in your academic career.* Sterling, VA: Stylus.

Hodges, S. (2001). Losing my way. In J. Kottler (Ed.), *Counselors finding their way* (pp. 77–80). Alexandria, VA: American Counseling Association.

Kadison, R., & DiGeronimo, T. F. (2004). *College of the overwhelmed: The campus mental health crisis and what to do about it.* San Francisco: Jossey-Bass.

Kübler-Ross, E. (1969). *On death and dying.* New York: Macmillan.

Lasley, M. (2004). *Courageous visions: How to unleash passionate energy in your life and your organization.* Burlington, PA: Discover Press.

Lippincott, J. A, & Lippincott, R. B. (2007). *Special populations in college counseling: A handbook for mental health professionals.* Alexandria, VA: American Counseling Association.

Moore, C. W. (2003). *The mediation process: Practical strategies for resolving conflict* (3rd ed.). San Francisco: Jossey-Bass.

Myers, I. B., & Myers, P. B. (1995). *Gifts differing*. Palo Alto, CA: Davies-Black.

National Board for Certified Counselors. (2009). *Continuing education*. Retrieved July 24, 2009, from http://www.nbcc.org/ContinuingEducation/counselors/default.aspx

No Child Left Behind Act of 2001, Pub. L. No. 107–110, 115 Stat. 1425 (2002).

Parker, Y. (2002). *The damn good résumé guide: A crash course in résumé writing*. Berkeley, CA: Ten Speed Press.

Pascarella, E. T., & Terenzini, P. T. (2005). *How college affects students: A third decade of research*. San Francisco: Jossey-Bass.

Perls, F. (1969). *Gestalt therapy verbatim*. Moab, UT: Real People Press.

Remley, T., & Herlihy, B. (2007). *Ethical, legal, and professional issues in counseling* (2nd ed.). Upper Saddle River, NJ: Merrill Prentice Hall.

Rokeach, M. (2000). *Understanding human values: Individual and societal*. New York: Simon & Schuster.

Seligman, M. E. P. (1998). *Learned optimism* (2nd ed.). New York: Pocket Books.

Singaravelu, H. D., & Pope, M. (Eds.). (2007). *A handbook for counseling international students in the United States*. Alexandria, VA: American Counseling Association.

TIME's man of the year. (2009). *Time*. Retrieved July 24, 2009, from http://history1900s.about.com/library/weekly/aa050400a.htm

U.S. Department of Labor, Bureau of Labor Statistics. (2008). *The occupational outlook handbook*. Washington, DC: Author. (Available at http://www.bls.gov/OCO/)

Walsh, R. J., & Dasenbrook, N. C. (2007). *The complete guide to private practice for licensed mental health professionals* (4th ed.). Rockford, IL: Crysand Press.

Walter, J. L., & Peller, J. E. (1992). *Becoming solution-focused in brief therapy*. New York: Brunner/Mazel.

Webster's dictionary and thesaurus of the English language. (1992). Danbury, CT: Lexicon.

Wooden, J. R. (2005). *Wooden on leadership*. New York: McGraw-Hill.